MEASURING TOURISM PERFORMANCE

Tzung-Cheng (T.C.) Huan

Joseph T. O'Leary

Champaign, Illinois
www.sagamorepub.com

Interior Layout: Michelle R. Dressen
Cover Design: Julie L. Denzer

ISBN:1-57167-260-5
Library of Congress Card Catalog Number: 99-62750

Printed in the United States of America.

Aim & Scope of Series

ADVANCES IN TOURISM APPLICATIONS provides a new forum for organizing and presenting emerging theory and management practices in five broadly defined areas of tourism management: (1) destination marketing, (2) destination management, (3) environment, (4) policy, and (5) statistics and theory. This new series of monographs attempts to fill an important gap between textbooks and journal articles, representing a comprehensive discussion of the most current theories and/or practices by leading scholars and industry professionals. Each volume identifies and discusses the most current theories and/or practices relevant to a specific topic, provides concrete examples and explanations of the importance of these theories/practices to the tourism industry, and provides extensive bibliographic resources.

As editors of the series, we want to encourage and facilitate the creativity of researchers and managers in tourism. Specifically, we invite readers to contribute by submitting manuscripts and/or case studies which describe innovative applications in the tourism industry. We welcome your ideas and suggestions for future topics and look forward to joining you on this journey of building knowledge for the 21st century.

Dr. Daniel R. Fesenmaier
Dept. of Leisure Studies
University of Illinois at
Urbana-Champaign
Champaign, IL USA

Dr. Joseph T. O'Leary
Dept. of Forestry &
Natural Resources
Purdue University
W. Lafayette, IN USA

Dr. Muzaffer S. Uysal
Dept. of Hospitality and
Tourism Management
Virginia Polytechnic Institute
Blacksburg, VA USA

Other titles currently available in the
Advances in Tourism Applications Series

VOLUME ONE
Measuring Tourism Performance
Tzung-Cheng (T.C.) Huan and Joseph O'Leary

VOLUME TWO
Making Visitors Mindful: Principles for Creating Quality Sustainable Visitor Experiences Through Effective Communication
Gianna Moscardo

VOLUME THREE
Tourism Policy: The Next Millennium
David L. Edgell, Sr.

VOLUME FOUR
Positioning Tourist Destinations
Allen Z. Reich

VOLUME FIVE
Tourism Service Satisfaction
Francis P. Noe

. . . .

Upcoming titles

VOLUME SIX
Meta-Evaluation: Achieving Effective Tourism Marketing Programs
Arch G. Woodside and Marcia Y. Sakai

VOLUME SEVEN
Entrepreneurship and Innovation in Tourism
Sustainable Community Tourism Development
Thomas D. Potts

VOLUME EIGHT
Entrepreneurship and Innovation in Tourism
Frank Go

VOLUME NINE
The Design Analysis and Improvement of Tourist Services
Eric Laws

VOLUME TEN
Tourism Destination Marketing: Organizations, Strategies, and Programs
Alastair Morrison

Contents

CHAPTER FOUR

Geographical/Population Indices

CHAPTER FIVE

Price/Economic Indices

1 Introduction

TRAVEL AND TOURISM INDICES

IN ORDER to better understand the dynamics of the travel and tourism industry and improve the direction of marketing programs, tourism professionals need to measure and monitor market changes. Identifying the travel and tourism market changes certainly can guide the development of improved marketing strategies. Index scores may be a useful tool to follow market changes and evolution.

Actually, index numbers are widely used in scientific research to observe events like stock market fluctuation, economic expectations, and biological and medical inspection. In agriculture and biology, index scores have been broadly applied to monitor fish (Minns, Cairns, and Randall, 1994) and waterbird populations (Underhill, 1994), to select cattle in dairy cattle breeding (Philipsson, Banos, and Arnason, 1994), to examine the effects of testosterone on skeletal growth in lambs (Peralta, Arnold, and Currie, 1994), and even to test a turf crop's resistance to water stress (Jalali-Farahani, Slack, and Kopec, 1994).

In the social sciences, the index-score concept has been utilized to inspect an infant's mental development (Cherny, Fulker, and Emde, 1994), to examine interpersonal reactivity (Hatcher, Nadeau, and Walsh, 1994), to identify the nonverbal language deficits of elementary school children (Love, Nowicki, and Duke, 1994), to predict mortality of nursing home patients (Frisoni, Franzoni, and Rozzini, 1994), and to measure therapeutic actions in psychotherapy (Weissmark and Giacomo, 1994).

In business and economics, index scores have been employed to monitor stock market fluctuation (Stevenson, 1995; *Wall Street Journal* [Eastern Edition], 1995), to describe employment cost changes (Uchitelle, 1995; Georges, 1995), to depict consumer prices (Dilts, 1994), and to forecast a country's economic power (Clayton-Matthews, Kodrzycki, and Swaine, 1994; *New York Times* [Late New York Edition], 1994).

In travel and tourism, the idea of an index score has also been broadly used to measure the attractiveness of touristic destinations (Gearing, et al., 1974; Tang and

Rochananond, 1991), to analyze tourists' travelling activities (Hogan and Rex, 1984; Keogh, 1984), and to examine travellers' spending for international tourism-demand estimation (Joseph and Judd, 1974; Witt and Martin, 1987; Uysal and Crompton, 1987; Morley, 1994).

DEFINITION AND IDEA OF AN INDEX SCORE

Before detailing the idea of an index score, it is necessary to provide a definition. According to *Webster's Ninth New Collegiate Dictionary* (Merriam-Webster Inc., 1983), index number means "a number used to indicate change in magnitude (cost or price) as compared with the magnitude at some specified time usually taken as 100." Bowley (1902) stated that "Index numbers are used to measure the change in some quantity which we cannot observe directly, which we know to have a definite influence on many other quantities which we can so observe, tending to increase all, or diminish all, while this influence is concealed by the actions of many causes affecting the separate quantities in various ways." Mendenhall and Reinmuth (1982) stated that index numbers are used to make meaningful comparisons over time.

> *An index number is a ratio or an average of ratios involving two or more time periods expressed as a percentage. One of the two time periods is usually a base time period, which serves as the standard point of comparison. The resulting score is, therefore, an average of relative values and not an average of the original data.*

From the above three definitions, index numbers are used to monitor a change of business by comparing the dynamic circumstances with a base object. Further, some indices were developed through a designed formula without reference to a base year or object. For example, the national tourism indicators developed by Statistics Canada (1996a) were simply the descriptive numbers for tourism demand and supply defined in dollars and adjusted or not adjusted for the seasonality. However, by comparing the indices across the time series (by season), tourism-market change in Canada can be successfully monitored and measured.

By knowing changes in index numbers, not only can further business expectations be predicted, but other influential factors can be discovered. Appraising the information generated from index scores can help managers and marketers develop more effective strategies to achieve their objectives.

SIMPLE VS. AGGREGATE (SIMPLE/WEIGHTED) INDICES

Backman, Uysal, and Backman (1992) declared that an index can be either "simple" or an "aggregate." Moreover, an "aggregate" index can also be either a "simple aggregate" index or a "weighted aggregate" index. First, a simple index is a ratio of an average measure in a year to the average measure in a base year. An example of a simple index would be the attendance at provincial parks in Ontario in 1997 divided by the attendance at provincial parks in Ontario in 1996 and multiplied by 100.

A simple aggregate index is the ratio of the sum of quantities or prices for a given year to the sum of the quantities or prices of the same items in some base year expressed as a percentage. An example of an aggregate index would be to sum the simple indices for all types of attractions in Ontario in 1997 (e.g., provincial parks, museums, city visitor centers) and divide that total by the number of attraction categories and multiply by 100. A weakness of the simple aggregate index is that changes in the measuring units may affect the value of the index. This weakness becomes a problem when trying to make meaningful comparisons.

Conversely, the weighted aggregate index is modified to provide a more uniform measure of comparison. In a weighted aggregate index, the values (or quantities) may not contribute equally to the value of the index since each value (or quantity) is multiplied (weighted) by the quantity or value of the items measured. Thus, the importance of each item in reference to the aggregate sum is considered in this index. Several of the indices used in the tourism industry fall into this category, since a weighting factor can be used to adjust for inflation and seasonality. As with the simple aggregate index, bias can be reduced by creating a geometric mean index, which involves a transformation of the values using the logarithm of the raw values.

All the indices mentioned above can be formulated as follows:

A. Simple index

$$\frac{\text{an average measure in a year}}{\text{the average measure in a base year}} * 100$$

B. Aggregate index

a. Simple aggregate index

$$\frac{\text{sum of values for a given year (unweighted)}}{\text{sum of values of the same items in some base year (unweighted)}} * 100$$

b. Weighted aggregate index

$$\frac{\text{sum of values for a given year (weighted)}}{\text{sum of values of the same items in some base year (weighted)}} * 100$$

TYPE AND USE OF TOURISM INDICES

Generally speaking, the index scores in tourism industry are to measure and monitor (1) regional tourism activity and (2) personal travel behavior. For measuring regional tourism activity, according to Backman, Uysal, and Backman (1992), the indices in travel and tourism can be categorized into four major groups: (1) Travel/Tourism Indices, (2) Trip Indices, (3) Consumer Price Indices (CPI), and (4) Miscellaneous Specific Purpose Indices.

Travel/Tourism Indices

Travel/Tourism Indices attempt to "provide a single number which can represent the changing level of activity in the area's tourism." Five of the commonly used Travel/Tourism Indices include: (1) the Tourist Function (TF), (2) the Travel Index (TI), (3) the Activity Index (AI), (4) the Travel Price Index (TPI), and (5) the Relative Price Index (RPI). All these are aggregate indices (Backman, Uysal, and Backman, 1992). The main difference is in the variable chosen to represent the measure of tourism.

Trip Indices

Trip Indices (TIs) are used to measure travel time. TIs relate the length of the stay in a country or at a destination to the total length of the trip (Pearce and Elliot, 1983; Uysal and McDonald, 1989). The data are generally obtained through a visitor survey. Although the Trip Index is a relative measure of time, it differs from the traditional concept of indices as used in economics in that it does not relate the measure to a base year. It can be considered a simple index measure since it is a non-aggregated, relative time score converted to a percentage.

Consumer Price Indices (CPI)

The third type of index, the present Consumer Price Index (CPI) formerly called the "Cost of Living," was initiated at the time of World War I for use in wage negotiation (United States Department of Labor, 1966). The CPI provides a commonly used measure of change in the aggregate price level of consumer goods and services. It yields timely information on price movements since it is available on a monthly basis and with a short time lag. Nonetheless, as an indicator of change in the cost of living, it is susceptible to various types of measurement bias (Crawford, 1993) arising from the fixed composition of the CPI basket, the exclusion of new goods from the current basket, the changing quality of products, and shifts in market share between high- and low-price retail outlets. Due to reliability problems of tourism data in many countries (other than Canada and the U.S.), an approximation is generally used, which is the Consumer Price Index (CPI) of the country under consideration. For example, Uysal and Crompton (1984) used the general consumer price index as the price of tourism service. Morley (1994) also verified that it was reasonable to use the Consumer Price Index (CPI) as a proxy for tourism prices in demand models because of their very high correlation.

Miscellaneous Specific Purpose Indices

Indices can also be generated for specific purposes, and some of the commonly used Travel/Tourism Indices are the (1) Country Potential Generation Index (CPGI), (2) Travel Propensity Index (TPI), (3) Net Travel Propensity (NTP), (4) Gross Travel Propensity (GTP), (5) Relative Acceptance Index (RA), (6) Room Comfort Index (RCI), and so on.

The indices can also be utilized to explore other information. Therefore, the use of multivariate analysis with indices is not unusual. For example, Huan (1997) developed seven groups of indices to monitor U.S. travellers in Canada and then utilized these indices to generate a model to explain U.S. travellers' behaviors. Moreover, factor components and regression also have been employed to analyze indices in the research areas of banking, finance, and economics (Silber, 1989; Chan and Chung, 1995; Antoniou and Holmes, 1995; Wei, 1995; Mezrich, 1994).

CONSIDERATIONS IN TOURISM INDICES

Major considerations in the development of travel and tourism indices are (1) seasonal variation, (2) the strength of the index, and (3) the data problem (Backman, et al., 1992).

Indices which are not adjusted for seasonality may lead to erroneous conclusions because seasonality of price level change and month-to-month seasonal variation may drastically affect tourist demand. Statistical measures can be used to overcome this variation and produce data which can be used in comparison studies. A non-seasonally adjusted index is generally referred to as a crude index. A crude index is seasonally adjusted by one of several methods. Three methods which have appeared in recent tourism studies are the (1) arithmetic mean, (2) X-11 Shishkin approach, and (3) X-11 ARIMA method.

Arithmetic mean was employed by Backman and Uysal (1987) to deseasonalize the seasonal variation. In their method, first, the arithmetic mean of the actual monthly data attendance at 97 state parks in Texas from 1978 to 1984 is computed. Next, the mean monthly totals are summed and divided by 12 to produce an overall average of monthly attendance. Once this is calculated, the average month is identified as equaling 100; thus, the base for the index is computed. Each of the monthly means is divided by the average monthly mean to produce the index of seasonal variation for the attendance across the data (see Table 1).

The X-11 Shishkin seasonal adjustment program was developed by Julius Shishkin, Young, and Musgrave (1976) in 1967 and was officially accepted by the U.S. Department of Commerce. The X-11 program was available for use with the SAS statistical package system (SAS Institute, 1980). Bond and McDonald (1978), Judd and Rulison (1983), Hogan and Rex (1984), and others have used this method for seasonal adjustment.

On the other hand, the X-11-ARIMA (Auto-Regressive Integrated Moving Average) method was developed by Dagum (1974) by modifying the X-11 Shishkin approach. This was officially adopted by Statistics Canada in January, 1975, for the

Month	Mean Monthly Demand	Index of Seasonal Variation (Average month = 100)
January	657,893	49.4
February	790,401	59.4
March	1,370,439	103.0
April	1,655,387	124.4
May	1,833,950	137.8
June	2,063,904	155.1
July	2,156,237	162.0
August	1,716,979	129.0
September	1,159,401	87.1
October	1,063,261	79.9
November	867,158	65.2
December	634,659	47.4
Average	1,330,806	100.0

*Data used to generate the index were obtained from Texas Tourism Development Agency, Attractions Data, 1984 (Backman and Uysal, 1987)

Table 1: An index of seasonal variation based on the arithmetic mean of actual monthly data attendance at 97 state parks in Texas, 1978–1984

seasonal adjustment of the main Labour Force series and other economic indicators (Statistics Canada, 1980). The X-11-ARIMA was also applied for the Canadian national tourism indicator development (Statistics Canada, 1996b). The advantage of the X-11-ARIMA adjustment are twofold. First, by carrying out the seasonal adjustment at the most detailed level, seasonal shifts in the aggregates are more easily explained. Second, the calculation of seasonally adjusted aggregates by summation preserves the accounting identifier in the system, which is much more convenient for users.

As for the strength of the index, it is possible to test the strength of an index using the Factors Test. This procedure tests whether the values from the original data differ from those using the index formula.

Data problems are prevalent in the travel and tourism field. One of the problems is lack of accurate data. The lack of standardization of data both by reporting agencies and by agencies computing indices becomes a major problem. Data are becoming more available and several agencies such as Statistics Canada, Pacific Area Travel Association (PATA), and World Tourism Organization (WTO) are attempting to collect and produce more reliable standardized data. Especially, Statistics Canada has collected several successful time-series data sets for which the information is preferred for developing indices.

SUMMARY AND IMPLICATIONS OF INDEX SCORES

Indices have been widely used in scientific research for various applications. Backman, Uysal, and Backman (1992) state that travel and tourism indices offer several management advantages to measure and compare a state or regional tourist activity, to assist in setting standards, for calculations which quickly show tourists' spending in term of a constant value, and for planning and projecting. Although they organized the major indices into four groups, some of the important measures are "masked" in the categories they employed. To overcome this problem, this book will discuss five major groups: (1) Hotel/Restaurant Indices, (2) Activity/Trip Indices, (3) Geographical/Population Indices, (4) Price/Economic Indices, and (5) Miscellaneous Indices. Depending on the situation the manager, planner, or researcher encounters, the information should provide the basis for formulating an index, or provide for the design of a variation to address the specific need.

2

Travel & Tourism Indices

INDEX NUMBERS, which are used to monitor a change of business by comparing the dynamic circumstances with a base object, are widely employed in scientific research to observe events such as stock market fluctuation, economic expectations, and medical inspection. The idea of index values is also popularly used in the travel industry. The advantages of these indices are that they provide opportunities to measure and compare regional tourist activity, to assist in setting standards, for calculations which quickly show tourist spending in terms of constant value, and for planning and projecting. Moreover, these indices can be used to compose graphical information that portray images and patterns of change in the travel and tourism market. However, the seasonal variation, the strength of the index, and the data problems (Backman, et al., 1992) have to be considered when the indices are developed, employed, or explained.

The measures developed in this book are divided into five major groups. The first section, Hotel/Restaurant Indices, focuses on both hotels and restaurants and presents measures that examine business opportunities and performance. The second section, Activity/Trip Indices, examines information about travel activity and programming at specific destinations. The third section, Geographical/Population Indices, is used by both public and private organizations. By examining a visitor population from different countries or political regions, the travel agency can understand the importance of the different market segments and then develop strategies directed at those markets. The fourth section, Price/Economic Indices, is the most significant for tourism economists and entrepreneurs to understand the consumption and economic contributions of their markets. The final section, called Miscellaneous Indices, explores different travel and tourism measures that are developed for a variety of specific applications.

Based on the functions and further applications of these indices in travel and tourism, the reader can consult those measures that appear most useful and develop their own applications for business or projects.

HOTEL/RESTAURANT INDICES

This section addresses the area of Hotel/Restaurant Indices. These are important to both the hotel and restaurant business because this set of measures provides insight into information about business opportunities and performance. In this group, the accommodation indices show an example about the importance levels of different types of accommodations for U.S. overnight pleasure travel parties who visited Ontario from the Great Lakes states (Huan, 1997). The investment performance indices are based on the ratio of return to risk and are measured by the return, or the reward, for each unit of the risk associated with the asset (Gu, 1994). The lodging index is a useful statistic because it reflects revenues per room, which is an important concern to industry practitioners, particularly for local travel destinations where average occupancy and room rates are not available (Wassenaar and Stafford, 1991).

The restaurant activity index is presented through an example about consumers' propensity to dine out in the 316 U.S. metropolitan market and indicates how inclined local residents are toward dining out (Restaurant Business Inc., 1994). The restaurant growth index shows the relationship between restaurant supply and demand as an index. What it includes is a market-by-market look at relevant consumer demographics such as disposable income, dining-out habits, and per-capita spending on restaurants and fast food (Restaurant Business, Inc., 1994). The R&D/NDS Restaurant Opportunity Index (ROI) is designed to highlight areas that offer the greatest potential for restaurant expansion (Chaudhry, Rogers, and Kosinski, 1994). The Room Comfort Index (RCI) has been used as a single comfort index for each location, and it examines comfort level in a single accommodation sector as a means of identifying regions or areas specializing in particular types of tourism (Mirloup, 1974).

The Spatial Association Index is a method for comparing point pattern distribution, and this index uses the logic of comparing an expected pattern to an observed pattern to reach a conclusion about the degree of clustering, dispersion, or randomness (Lee, 1979). The Tourism Function of an area is a measure of tourism activity or identity reflected by the visitor and the visited; the index is derived by comparing the number of beds available to tourists in the area with the resident population of the area (Defert, 1967). Different from Defert's TF, the Tourist Intensity is calculated by comparing the total number of tourist nights in each county with their resident populations. This reflects the intensity of use, i.e., the average number of visitor bednights per unit per year (Keogh, 1984; Potts and Uysal, 1992). All the original ideas, technical formula, statistical outputs, and applications of the indices in this Hotel/Restaurant Indices group will be detailed in the following section.

Accommodation Index

The accommodation index was developed by Huan (1997) to measure and monitor the accommodations used by U.S. Great Lakes region overnight pleasure travel parties in Ontario, Canada. In the study the data were collected by Statistics Canada in conducting the Canadian International Travel Survey (for the travel parties from other countries). The accommodation index for different types of accommodations used was defined as follows:

Specific accommodation stayed in—Yes : No = 100 : 0
*The Accommodation Index could be of (1) hotel, (2) motel, (3) home of friends/relatives, (4) camping/trailer park, (5) cottage/cabin, and (6) other.

These Accommodation Indices show the importance levels of different types of accommodations for U.S. overnight pleasure travel parties who visited Ontario from the Great Lakes states. In Table 2 and Figure 1, "Hotel" was the most important accommodation used, especially in the fall and winter (from October to March).

	Hotel	Motel	Home of F/R	Camp	Cottage/ Cabin	Other
1990 Jan-Mar	55.00	28.11	6.32	0.89	8.48	4.75
1990 Apr-Jun	39.28	24.79	4.45	7.73	27.56	4.58
1990 Jul-Sep	33.87	30.16	4.48	13.46	22.20	5.20
1990 Oct-Dec	51.86	22.72	12.88	1.26	11.43	4.37
1991 Jan-Mar	57.65	22.90	6.41	0.54	6.29	3.95
1991 Apr-Jun	31.55	22.94	6.15	13.97	29.00	5.46
1991 Jul-Sep	28.44	23.98	5.57	13.76	22.83	4.39
1991 Oct-Dec	57.97	23.84	6.61	2.18	10.88	5.14
1992 Jan-Mar	61.17	26.43	5.54	0.00	8.19	0.38
1992 Apr-Jun	43.09	24.77	3.32	7.45	23.11	3.68
1992 Jul-Sep	34.30	19.86	7.61	11.95	27.02	6.80
1992 Oct-Dec	53.70	24.43	10.44	1.47	11.98	4.23
1993 Jan-Mar	63.12	17.68	13.20	0.10	5.22	3.20
1993 Apr-Jun	33.96	23.74	4.71	8.87	29.19	5.97
1993 Jul-Sep	37.01	23.51	5.08	9.03	26.48	5.40
1993 Oct-Dec	55.46	20.03	8.05	1.76	12.48	5.10
1994 Jan-Mar	58.17	20.83	7.56	0.66	9.26	5.11
1994 Apr-Jun	42.52	22.40	5.52	7.43	22.03	6.67
1994 Jul-Sep	38.73	25.94	5.04	12.21	21.40	8.88
1994 Oct-Dec	57.30	14.75	7.36	0.87	8.05	10.99
1995 Jan-Mar	54.63	21.95	7.25	0.49	10.76	3.15
1995 Apr-Jun	41.39	20.34	4.11	8.32	24.71	7.85
1995 Jul-Sep	35.36	25.32	4.49	15.91	21.11	8.14
1995 Oct-Dec	57.41	15.05	7.18	0.64	12.57	9.75

Source: Huan, 1997

Table 2: Accommodation index of U.S. Great Lakes region travellers in Ontario

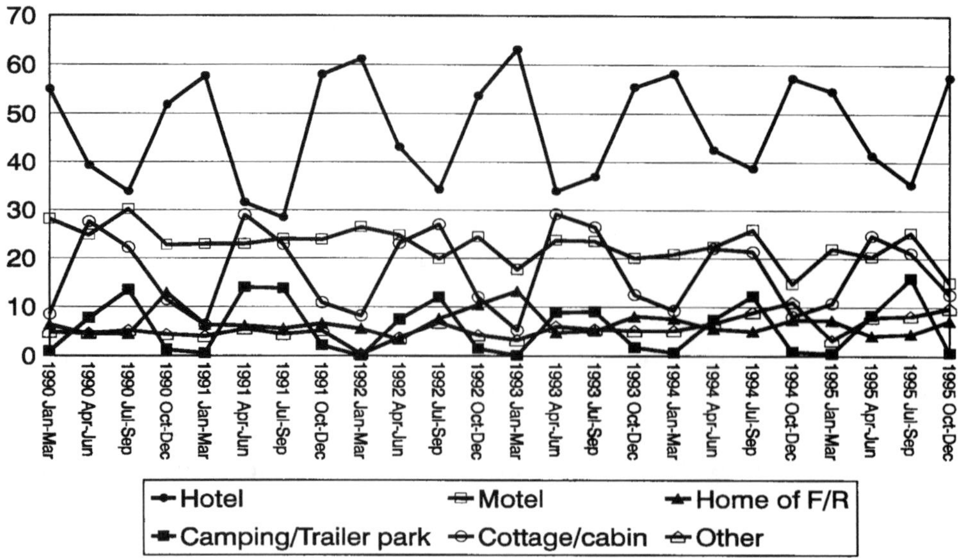

Generally speaking, the importance levels of "Hotel" increases in fall and winter but decreases in spring and summer while the importance levels of "cottage or cabin" and "Camping" increase in spring and summer but decrease in fall and winter.
Source: Huan, 1997

Figure 1: Accommodation index of U.S. Great Lakes region travellers in Ontario

"Motel" was the second most important accommodation, and the seasonal changes of its importance level were not significant. "Cottage/Cabin" was the third most important accommodation type, especially in spring and summer (from April to September). "Camping" was the fourth most important accommodation for these Great Lakes travellers, and its seasonal change was very similar to "Cottage/Cabin."

Investment Performance Index

The investment performance indices are based on the ratio of return to risk and are measured by the return, or the reward, for each unit of the risk associated with the asset (Gu, 1994). For a risk-averse investor, utility is determined by two factors: return and the variability, or the risk, of return. An asset with a higher return-to-risk ratio is superior to one with a lower return-to-risk ratio.

There are two types of risks that are relevant to the investor (Gu, 1994). First, when the investor holds a single investment asset, the utility is determined by the mean and standard deviation of the return. The standard deviation, also denoted as total risk, is the relevant risk. Secondly, if the investor diversifies by holding many different assets, then the relevant risk is the asset's covariance with the capital market. This covariance risk is denoted as systematic risk or nondiversifiable risk.

There are two types of performance indexes based on the ratio of return to risk. The performance index developed by Sharpe (1966), $PI_{s,}$ is:

$$PI_S = \frac{(ER_i - r)}{a_i}$$

where *PIs* is the investment performance index by Sharp (1966),
ERi is the mean return of the ith asset,
r represents the risk-free return,
ai is the standard deviation of the return of the ith asset.

Since the numerator is the asset's return in excess of risk-free return, this performance index actually measures a risky investment's excess return per unit of risk (standard deviation) of the "*i*th" risky investment. The risk variable used in this performance measure is the standard deviation of return, or the total risk of the investment. The underlying assumption of Sharpe's performance measure is that the investor holds only "one risky asset." The investor does not diversify or does not diversify completely across assets. Thus, the total risk is the risk the investor must bear and be rewarded for.

The reward-to-volatility ratio proposed by Treynor (1965) as a performance index of risky investment is different from Sharpe's index in the use of risk variable. Treynor's index is denoted as:

$$PI_T = \frac{(ER_i - r)}{b_i}$$

where PI_T is the investment performance index by Treynor (1965),
ER_i is the mean return of the ith asset,
r represents the risk-free return,
b_i is the systematic risk of the ith risky asset

Treynor's performance measure is similar to Sharpe's performance index in that it measures the risky asset's excess return per unit of risk. The risk variable used, however, is different. Sharpe's measure uses the risky asset's total risk, or the standard deviation, while Treynor's measure uses the systematic risk, or beta. The underlying assumption of Treynor's performance is that the investor holds "many different assets," and the unsystematic risk can be diversified away completely. Only the systematic risk is the relevant risk that the investor must bear and be rewarded for. Higher PI_T indicates better portfolio performance, because for each unit of systematic risk, the investor is rewarded with greater excess of return.

Gu (1994) applied both Sharpe's performance index and Treynor's performance index on his hospitality industry research. The risk and return features of the three sectors of the hospitality and S&P 500 are presented in Table 3; moreover, the numbers are used to calculate both Sharpe's and Treynor's performance indices. The results of Sharpe's index, PI_s, and Treynor's index, PI_T, of each sector and the S&P 500 is presented in Table 4. For the overall

	S&P 500	HOTEL	CASINO	RESTAURANT
		1983–1992		
Mean	0.0070	0.0039	0.0120	0.0079
Std Deviation	0.0350	0.0781	0.0781	0.0533
Beta ( )	1.0000	1.7140	1.5430	1.1680
		1987–1989		
Mean	0.0058	0.0090	0.0189	0.0045
Std Deviation	0.0411	0.0659	0.0726	0.0483
Beta ( )	1.0000	1.2330	1.3690	0.9680
		1990–1992		
Mean	0.0013	-0.0163	0.0096	0.0035
Std Deviation	0.0359	0.1132	0.0845	0.0617
Beta ( )	1.0000	2.6530	1.9770	1.4890

Source: Gu, 1994

Table 3: Return and risk of hospitality investment

	S&P 500	HOTEL	CASINO	RESTAURANT
		1983–1992		
PI_s	0.0933	0.0016	0.1110	0.0789
PI_T	0.0032	0.0001	0.0053	0.0036
		1987–1989		
PI_s	0.0681	0.0908	0.2174	0.0307
PI_T	0.0028	0.0049	0.011	0.0015
		1990–1992		
PI_s	-0.0198	-0.1632	0.0908	0.0253
PI_T	-0.0007	-0.0069	0.0038	0.0010

Source: Gu, 1994

Table 4: Hospitality investment performance indices

1983–1992 period, the casino portfolio, with a PI_s of 0.1110 and a PI_T of 0.0053, outperformed the other two sectors and the S&P 500 as well. The hotel sector, with a PIs of 0.0016 and a PI_T of 0.0001, was the worst among all the groups. The restaurant sector's two performance indices was inferior to that for the casino's, but its PI_T were superior to those of the S&P 500.

Lodging Index

The lodging index is defined as the average nightly revenue realized from each room, vacant or occupied, within a given region or city during a given time period (Wassenaar and Stafford, 1991). The lodging index is a useful statistic because it reflects revenues per room, which is an important concern to industry practitioners. The lodging index can be particularly useful for local travel destinations where average occupancy and room rates are not available. To determine the lodging index from transient occupancy tax information (LI_T), three components are needed: (1) total transient occupancy taxes collected, (2) the transient occupancy tax rate, and (3) hotel/motel room capacity. The first two components are public information, obtainable from local government finance departments. An inventory of hotel/motel room capacity is usually available from local convention/visitor bureaus or can be compiled without much difficulty. The formula for LI_T is:

$$LI_T = \frac{T}{t * C}$$

where LI_T is the lodging index,
T is the total transient occupancy taxes collected for the period,
t is transient occupancy tax rate for the period,
C is the room-night capacity for the period (number of rooms * number of nights),

When the number of rooms and/or the tax rate changes during a given time period, weighted averages of each component must be substituted into the equation. When assessing a region with more than one tax rate, such as a county or small region, the LI_T formula is:

$$LI_T = \frac{S\sum_{i=1}^{n} \frac{T_i}{t_i}}{S\sum_{i=1}^{n} C_i}$$

where LI_T is the lodging index,
T_i transient occupancy tax collections,

ti transient occupancy tax rate,
Ci number of room-nights available.

The lodging index can also be calculated as the product of (1) the average occupancy rate and (2) the average room rate of all occupied rooms:

$$LI_e = O * R$$

where *O* is the average occupancy rate,
R is the average room rate of all occupied rooms.

LI_T = Can be demonstrated as follows. Total spending on hotel/motel rooms (S) is equal to the transient occupancy taxes collected (T) divided by the tax rate (t). It is also equal to the product of the average occupancy rate (O), the room-night capacity (C), and the average occupied room rate (R).

Step 1. $$S = \frac{T}{t} = O * C * R$$

By definition, the lodging index is the average revenue per room-night, which is derived by dividing spending on hotel/motel rooms (S) by room-night capacity (C).

Step 2. $$LI = \frac{S}{C}$$

Substitute spending on hotel/motel rooms (S) with its equivalents shown in equation 1,

Step 3. $$LI = \frac{T/t}{C} = \frac{O * C * R}{C}$$ and simplify:

Step 4. $$LI = \frac{T}{t * C} = O * R$$

The LI_T's practical use is limited to smaller areas, such as cities or counties. Deriving LI_T for larger regions, such as a state or the nation, will be very difficult because of the complexities of accurately assessing various tax data and room counts. Thus, for large geographic areas where average occupancy and room-rate estimates are usually available, the LI_e formula will be more practical.

A case application of lodging index was developed by Wassenaar (1989) for Escondido, California. In Figure 2, the steady decline of the LI_T within the city of

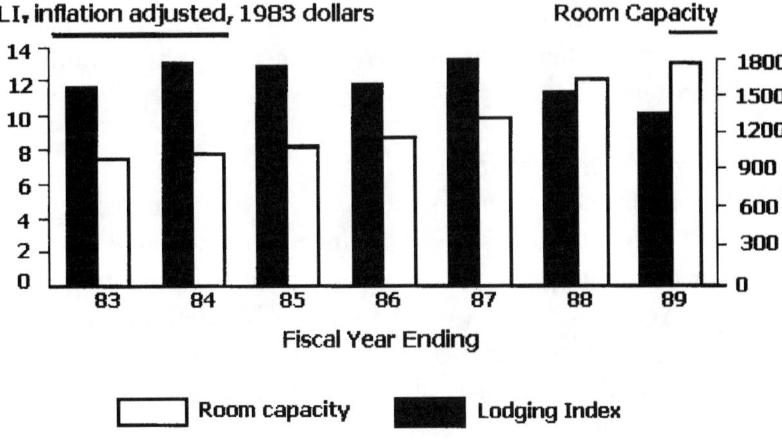

Source: Wassenaar, 1989

Figure 2: Lodging index vs. room capacity, city of Escondido

Metro Area	RGI	Rank
Champaign-Urbana	219	1
Muncie	195	2
Wichita Falls	185	3
La Crosse	183	4
Anniston	179	5
Lubbock	177	6
Honolulu	176	7
Raleigh-Durham-Chapel Hill	172	8
Lansing-East Lansing	171	9
Santa Fe	167	10
Merced	55	312
Redding	55	313
Vineland-Millville-Bridgeton	52	314
Yuba City	48	315
Visalia-Tulare-Porterville	46	316
United States Total	100	

Source: Restaurant Business, Inc., September 20, 1994

Table 5: 1993 restaurant activity index

Escondido was attributable to expansion of room capacity along the freeway corridors leading to the city. Room capacity for the greater Escondido area increased from 1,175 during fiscal year 1985-1986 to 1,763 during fiscal year 1988-1989. Because visitor volume remained relatively stable, the average revenue per available room-night dropped.

Restaurant Growth Index (RGI)

Building upon more than a quarter-century of accumulated statistical data, the Restaurant Growth Index is a well grounded and comprehensive market-selection tool. The restaurant growth index's geographic and demographic information features extensive statistical data on the U.S.'s 316 Metropolitan Areas and 211 Designated Market Areas. Included is a market-by-market look at relevant consumer demographics such as disposable income, dining-out habits, and per capita spending on restaurants and fast food.

The Restaurant Growth Index shows the relationship between restaurant supply and demand as an index (Restaurant Business, Inc., 1994). When supply equals demand, the index is 100. The amount by which the RGI exceeds 100 represents growth potential. When the market is saturated, the index drops below 100. The 1993 Restaurant Growth Index (Restaurant Business, Inc., 1993) is presented in Table 6, and the formula of the Restaurant Growth Index is as follows:

Metro Area	RGI	Rank
Brazoria	147	1
Decatur, Ala	135	2
Houston	135	3
Lake Charles	135	4
Minneapolis–St. Paul	135	5
Huntsville	129	6
Baton Rouge	126	7
Fort Worth–Arlington	126	8
Anniston	125	9
Greeley	124	10
San Luis Obispo–Atascadero–Paso Robles	61	312
Glens Falls	55	313
Enid	54	314
Barnstable–Yarmouth	50	315
Myrtle Beach	45	316
United States Total	100	

Source: Restaurant Business, Inc., September 20, 1994

Table 6: 1993 restaurant growth index

$$RGI = \frac{D}{S} * 100$$

where *D* is the restaurant demand, measured by eight factors: market's number of employed persons; market's number of working women; market's number of households with incomes of $25,000-$34,999; market's number of households with incomes of $35,000-$49,999; market's number of households with incomes of $50,000 or more; market's share of eating place sales; market's share of population age 18 and under, and 25-44 years of age; market's share of food consumed outside home,

S is the restaurant supply, measured by the percentage of total U.S. dining places located in the market.

Restaurant Opportunity Index (ROI)

The R&D/NDS Restaurant Opportunity Index (ROI) is designed to highlight the areas of the United States that offer the greatest potential for restaurant expansion (Chaudhry, Rogers, and Kosinski, 1994). With the support of San Diego-based Equifax National Decision Systems, a leader in the field of geographic and demographic target market, Chaudhry, Rogers, and Kosinski (1994) developed the model of Restaurant Opportunity Index that identifies metropolitan markets in which demand for restaurant dining is high—relative to regional averages—and restaurant numbers are low. The Restaurant Opportunity Index market analysis involves seven key variables:

1. supply measures:

   a. Number of eating and drinking locations,
   b. Total eating- and drinking-place sales, and
   c. Sales per location.

2. demand measures:

   d. Number of households,
   e. Estimated median income per household,
   f. Annual per-household expenditure on eating and drinking away from home, and
   g. Share of household income spent on eating and drinking away from home.

An index score of 100 marks the average for each region. The higher the ROI, the better the potential for new restaurants. The Restaurant Opportunity Index for each MSA is a function of income share and sales per location. The results of the Restaurant Opportunity Index study by Chaudhry, Rogers, and Kosinski (1994) are presented in Table 7 and the formula is as follows:

$$ROI = \frac{MSA_D}{D} * \frac{MSA_I}{I} * 100$$

where *ROI* is Restaurant Opportunity Index,
MSA is the Metropolitan Statistical Area and is defined by the Census Bureau as a city which, with contiguous densely settled territory, has a population of at least 50,000. If the MSA's largest city is smaller than 50,000, the area must support a total population of at least 100,000. MSAs typically include all surrounding counties with strong economic and social ties to the central city,
MSAD is MSA demand per location,
MSAI is MSA income share,
D is region's demand per location,
I is region's income share.

Room Comfort Index (RCI)

The Room Comfort Index (RCI) has been used as a single comfort index for each location and it examines comfort level in a single accommodation sector as a

			Eating and drinking locations					
Region	ROI	A (000)	B (000)	C (000)	D (000000)	E	F (000)	G
1. West South Central	127	3,298	$30	14	$5,783	$1,734	$407	5.76%
2. East South Central	126	3,171	31	14	5,726	1,736	404	5.73
3. South Atlantic	117	11,818	31	54	21,515	1,735	379	5.70
4. Mountain	110	3,990	34	19	7,269	1,822	381	5.32
5. West North Central	102	4,338	37	21	8,055	1,857	377	5.01
6. East North Central	93	12,689	34	67	23,790	1,774	325	5.27
7. Pacific	91	13,761	37	80	26,370	1,819	331	5.04
8. Middle Atlantic	89	13,119	35	77	25,147	1,781	310	5.29
9. New England	85	4,300	38	24	8,359	1,829	318	4.89
U.S. Totals	100	97,708	34	516	179,921	1,841	348	5.30

A. 1994 estimation households; B. 1994 median income; C. Locations; D. 1994 total sales; E. Per household expenditure; F. Demand per location; G. Income share
Source: Chaudhry, Rogers, and Kosinski (1994)

Table 7: Restaurant opportunities index by region

means of identifying regions or of identifying areas specializing in particular types of tourism. Mirloup (1974) prefers a single comfort index for each locality based on the formula

$$RCI = \frac{(0.25R_1 + 0.5R_2 + 0.75R_3 + R_4)}{TC} * 100$$

where *RCI* = Room Comfort Index
R1 to *R4* = the number of rooms in 1 to 4 star hotels
TC = total capacity of the resort or town

Spatial Association Index

The Spatial Association Index, developed by Lee (1979), is a method for comparing point pattern distribution. This index uses the logic of comparing an expected pattern to an observed pattern to reach a conclusion about the degree of clustering, dispersion, or randomness. The Spatial Association Index compares the distribution of one set of points to the distribution of a second set. The formula for the Spatial Association Index is:

$$R^* = \frac{d_o}{dr} \text{ and } d_r = \frac{m_1}{2[\sqrt{(n_2/a)}]} + \frac{m_2}{2[\sqrt{(n_1/a)}]}$$

where *do* is the mean distance obtained by (1) totaling all the distance between each point in the set studied and its nearest neighbor in the reference set of points, and (2) being divided by the number of points in the study set.
n1 is the number of points in set 1,
n2 is the number of points in set 2,
m1 is the relative proportion of set 1 to total; n1/(n1 + n2),
m2 is the relative proportion of set 1 to total; n2/(n1 + n2),
a is the area square units.

The values of the Spatial Association Index range from 0.00 and up. A value of 1.00 indicates a random distribution, values significantly less than 1.00 indicate clustering of one set of points with reference to the other set, values significantly greater than 1.00 indicate spatial avoidance.

The usefulness of the Spatial Association Index might be seen in a simple example given by Smith (1995). While analyzing the distribution of fast-food franchises in a large urban area, assumed that the outlets of one chain, “Bubba’s Burgers,” tend to avoid locating near other outlets of the same chain, but seek locations close to competitors from other chains (see Figure 3). The Spatial Association Index can differentiate the pattern of Bubba’s in comparison to other fast-food outlets and the calculation is as follows:

$$R^{*} = \frac{d_o}{d_r} = \frac{0.62}{1.54} = 0.40$$

$$\text{and } d_r = \frac{m_1}{2[\sqrt{(n_2/a)}]} + \frac{m_2}{2[\sqrt{(n_1/a)}]} = \frac{0.28}{2[\sqrt{(13/59.29)}]} + \frac{0.72}{2[\sqrt{(5/59.29)}]} = 1.54$$

where *do* is the mean distance obtained by (1), totaling all the distance between each point in the set studied and its nearest neighbor in the reference set of points, 0.4, 0.3, 1.2, 0.5, 0.7 units and (2) being divided by the number of points in the study set, 5.
n1 is the number of points in set 1,
n2 is the number of points in set 2,
m1 is the relative proportion of set 1 to total; $n_1/(n_1 + n_2)$,
m2 is the relative proportion of set 1 to total; $n_2/(n_1 + n_2)$,
a is the area square units.

Tourism Function (TF)

The Tourism Function was developed by Defert in 1967. The Tourism Function of an area is a measure of tourism activity or identity as reflected by the visitor and the visited. The index is derived by comparing the number of beds available to tourists in the area with the resident population of the area. The formula is as follows:

$$T(f) = \frac{N * 100}{P}$$

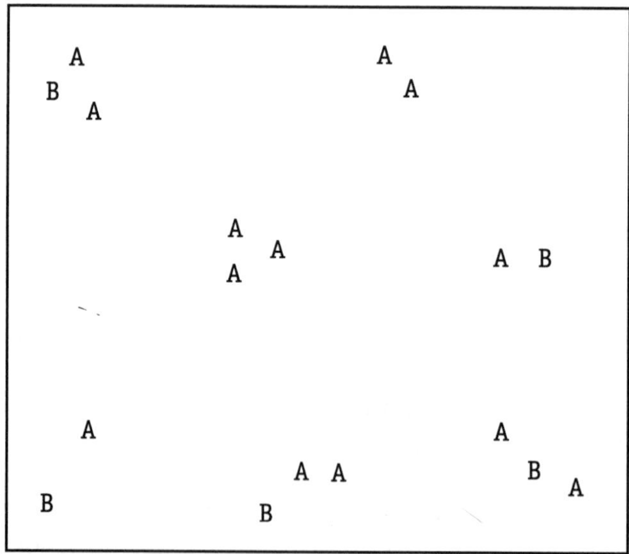

B = Bubba's Burgers
A = All other restaurants

Figure 3: Hypothetical pattern of fast-food restaurants

where N is the number of beds available to tourists,
P is the resident population of the area.

The theoretical limits of the index are T(f) = 0 where no tourist accommodation exists and T(f) = infinity where there is no resident population. A value of 100 indicates that the number of tourists would equal the number of local residents, assuming all beds available to tourists were being used (Pearce, 1995: 84).

Boyer (1972) proposes a six-fold classification of French communes based on their T(f) values:

T(f) >500 = recent "hypertouristic" resort
T(f) 100-500 = large tourist resort
T(f) 40-100 = predominantly tourist commune
T(f) 10-40 = communes with an important but not predominant tourist activity
T(f) 4-10 = little tourist activity or tourist function 'submerged' in other urban functions
T(f) <4 = practically no tourist activity.

The T(f) Index provides a useful complement to the traditional absolute capacity figure and has been successfully applied for regions in Colorado (Thompson, 1971), Normandy (Clary, 1977), New Brunswick (Keogh, 1984), Ontario (Hinch, 1990), and coastal South Carolina (Potts and Uysal, 1992). Keogh's case study (1984) in New Brunswick will be detailed in next paragraph.

Keogh (1984) employed Defert's index and looked at the problems of using physical accommodation capacity figures to identify spatial variations in the level of tourist activity. An analysis of accommodation use patterns in New Brunswick, Canada, shows considerable differences in the intensity of use among the various forms of accommodation. A closer look at hotel and motel occupancy characteristics also reveals large spatial variations. But their combined effect on the relationship between physical accommodation capacity and yearly tourist use shows little variation over space. It is concluded that Defert's index is the most useful tool for examining tourist activity in areas where most accommodation is in the form of hotels and motels. However, it should be interpreted with caution where there are large spatial variations in the types of accommodation available. Part of T(f) developed by Keogh (1984) is shown in Table 8.

Tourist Intensity (TI)

Tourist Intensity is a measure of the relative importance of tourism to the local economy (Keogh, 1984). Different from Defert's TF, the Tourist Intensity is calculated by comparing the total number of tourist nights in each county with their resident populations. It reflects the intensity of use (Potts and Uysal, 1992), the average number of visitor bednights per unit per year. The formula is:

County	Hotels/Motels (beds)		Cottage (beds)		Camping (places)		Total Capacity		Popu-lation (1976)	TF Value	Rank among County TF Values
	No.	%	No.	%	No.	%	No.	%			
Albert	567	11	1952	37	22709	52	5228	100	21946	23.8	6
Carleton	900	26	1376	39	1209	35	3485	100	24220	14.4	12
Charlotte	2424	23	5624	53	2502	24	10550	100	25042	42.1	2
Gloucester	2358	16	8256	57	3933	27	14547	100	79827	18.2	9
Kent	309	3	8148	83	1398	14	9855	100	28727	34.3	3
King's	651	5	8128	65	3651	30	12430	100	43137	28.8	4
Madawaska	1770	21	3776	45	2886	34	8432	100	34511	24.4	5
Northumberland	891	11	5264	62	2286	27	8441	100	53134	15.9	10
Queen's	336	3	5640	57	3915	40	9891	100	12564	78.7	1
Restigouche	1320	24	2748	50	1446	26	5514	100	40072	13.8	13
St. John	4236	51	3092	37	945	12	8273	100	87039	9.5	14
Sunbury	225	15	1252	75	153	10	1660	100	20668	8.0	15
Victoria	915	30	1504	50	579	20	2998	100	20588	14.6	11
Westmorland	5574	25	10200	46	6321	29	22095	100	102617	21.5	8
York	3777	25	7504	49	4062	26	15343	100	70433	21.8	7
Province of N.B.	26283	19	74464	54	37995	27	138742	100	664525	20.9	

Source: Keogh, 1984

Table 8: Defert's index of Canada

$$T(I) = \frac{n * 100}{P}$$

Where *n* is the number of tourist group bednights,
P is the resident population of the area.

The difference between the Tourism Function T(f) and Tourism Intensity T(I) is that when the Tourism Function is calculated in its simplest form [(number of beds/population) * 100], the index overestimates the intensity of tourism in low population areas. However, when the Tourist Intensity is weighted by the level of utilization [(number of visitor bednights/ population) * 100], intensity is more accurately reflected.

The TI Index provides a useful complement to the traditional, absolute-capacity figure and has been successfully applied for regions in New Brunswick (Keogh, 1984) and coastal South Carolina (Potts and Uysal, 1992). Both case studies in New Brunswick and coastal South Carolina will be briefly discussed in the next two paragraphs.

Keogh (1984) looked at the problems of using physical accommodation capacity figures to identify spatial variations in the level of tourist activity in New Brunswick, Canada. By comparing the total number of tourist nights in each county with their resident population, the TI is a measure of the relative importance of tourism to the local economy in New Brunswick. In the study, the results and the calculation of the estimate number of tourist bednights for hotels and motels are presented in Table 9.

Potts and Uysal (1992) also used Tourist Intensity to analyze the spatial composition of the tourism supply resources with special reference to accommodations in the eight coastal counties of South Carolina. In the study, the supply resources included hotels/motels, campgrounds and campsites, villas, eating and drinking establishments, and recreation attractions. Then, the total supply (total visitor bednights) were estimated based on the daily expenditure patterns per party and total travel generated expenditures.

County	Accommo-dation Capacity		Avail-ability Rate		Occu-pancy Rate		Propor-tion of Tourists		Annual no. of tourist Bednights	Popu-lation	TI (H)	Rank
Albert	567	x	122	x	.64	x	.95	=	42058	21946	192	9
Carleton	900		347		.60		.41		76825	24220	317	7
Charlotte	2424		233		.49		.61		168816	25042	674	1
Gloucester	2358		355		.61		.36		183825	79827	230	8
Kent	309		247		.48		.50		18317	28727	64	13
King's	651		291		.70		.54		71608	43137	166	11
Madawaska	1770		363		.55		.32		113081	34511	328	6
Northumberland	891		362		.68		.36		78958	53134	149	12
Restigouche	1320		342		.69		.22		68528	40072	171	10
St. John	4236		340		.70		.34		342777	87039	394	4
Victoria	915		347		.60		.41		78106	20588	379	5
Westmorland	5574		321		.68		.35		425842	102617	415	3
York	3777		351		.74		.31		304121	70433	431	2
Province of N.B.	25692		324		.64		.37		1972862	631293	312	

*Physical accommodation capacity means number of rooms/beds, availability rate means number of days accommodation open in a year, and proportion of tourists (-> among hotel, motel clientele) means.

**Excluding the counties of Queen's (336 beds) and Sunbury (225 beds) for which complete data were not available.

Source: Keogh, 1984

Table 9: Tourist intensity of Canada

3

Activity/Trip Indices

ACTIVITY/TRIP INDICES are useful to travel marketers because they provide information about travel activity and activity programming in a specific destination. The Activity Index represents an aggregate index that measures relative change in tourism activity; therefore, tourism activity (attendance) data at given locations over a period of time are used as a measure of the tourism level (Backman and Uysal, 1987, 1992; Tierney, 1990). The Destination Diversification Index is an indicator of activity compatibility (and the role travel strategies play) used for facility or site planning. This is accomplished by comparing the number of facilities at which one recreates (the degree of activity concentration or diversification) to the number of recreation activities in which one participates (Fesenmaier and Lieber, 1988).

The Main Activity Index is developed to monitor the importance level of various activities participated in by travel parties at a destination (Huan, 1997). The Tourism Barometer provides a measure of the relative changes in tourist activity over time. At the national level in the U.S., it was used by the U.S. Travel Data Center (USTDC); at the regional level, it was applied to examine regional activity by using different criteria. The concept of travel frequency refers to the average number of trips taken by a person participating in travel in a given period (Schmidhauser, 1975). Trip Indices are used to measure travel time, and the indices relate the length of stay in a country or at a destination to the total length of trip (Pearce and Elliot, 1983; Uysal and McDonald, 1989; Huan, 1997). All the original ideas, technical formula, statistical outputs, and applications of the indices in this Activity/Trip Indices group will be detailed in the following part of this section.

Activity Index

Backman and Uysal (1992) claim that the index employed by Backman and Uysal (1987) and Tierney (1990) is an Activity Index and represents an aggregate index that measures relative change in tourism activity. Tourism activity (attendance) data at given locations over a period of time are used as a measure of the tourism level.

Generally speaking, the Activity Index described above is a type of Tourism Barometer. One example of a Tourism Barometer at the national level is developed by the U.S. Travel Data Center (USTDC), now part of the Tourism Industry Association (TIA). At the regional level, Bond and McDonald (1978) state that their Arizona Tourism Barometer could be developed in the form of (1) dollar expenditures or (2) activity levels. However, for budget reasons, only the activity level was employed. This Arizona Tourism Barometer, which used an activity level (attendance), is called *Activity Index* by Backman and Uysal (1992).

One of the reference formulas developed by Bond and McDonald (1978) for Arizona is as follows:

$$I = \sum_{L=1}^{n} \frac{\text{Activity (L, QTR)}}{\text{Activity (L, Base)/4}} * \text{Weight (L)}$$

The above equation is used in calculating the index for a given location for the current quarter. Each activity sample stratum is weighted according to its relative quantity in the base year. Comparison of the current quarter with the average quarter in the base year produces a value that includes seasonal variation. Moreover, Bond and McDonald (1978) employed Shishkin's seasonality factors to deseasonalize the activity levels for the current quarter to generate a seasonally adjusted index value.

In the Arizona case study, the seasonality factors are estimated from the 1972–1976 database for each location. The average Activity Index value of the base year 1976 is 100. The result is detailed in Table 10. According to Backman and Uysal (1992), the strength of the Activity Index is to help monitor activity change over time for a given attraction. However, the weakness of the Activity Index is that it does not differentiate between visitor types, does not include the local population, and does not use distance in calculations. The benefits of the Activity Index (Tourism Barometer) are that indices are quickly useful in a short time, and it can also be published at intervals (monthly, quarterly, and annual variations are all possible) depending on the data input.

Destination Diversification Index

The Destination Diversification Index was developed by Fesenmaier and Lieber (1988) as an indicator of activity compatibility for facility or site planning. Therefore, for planning purposes, any study attempting to define outdoor recreation activity packages should assume resource dependency. Conceptually, it appears that one can investigate activity compatibility (and the role travel strategies play) by comparing the number of facilities at which one recreates (the degree of activity concentration or diversification) to the number of recreation activities in which one participates.

Year	Quarter	Raw Index		Seasonally Adjusted Index	
1972	I	63.51		71.14	
	II	72.46		70.90	
	III	86.06		77.35	
	IV	76.65	(u = 74.7)	78.72	(u = 74.5)
1973	I	63.97		82.37	
	II	99.18		84.63	
	III	103.68		82.08	
	IV	65.05	(u = 83.0)	82.47	(u = 82.9)
1974	I	55.49		72.12	
	II	92.66		77.87	
	III	100.33		80.56	
	IV	69.92	(u = 79.6)	88.38	(u = 79.7)
1975	I	71.44		93.22	
	II	103.90		87.94	
	III	115.91		91.20	
	IV	74.02	(u = 91.3)	91.32	(u = 90.9)
1976	I	78.40		101.12	
	II	120.93		102.06	
	III	119.63		94.31	
	IV	81.04	(u = 100)	99.76	(u = 99.3)
1977	I	100.82		124.53	
	II	123.36		104.23	
	III	131.22		102.73	
	IV	89.14	(u = 111.1)	111.59	(u = 110.7)
1978	I	93.94		119.62	
	II	131.14		110.21	

Activity Index (Arizona Tourism Barometer: 1976 = 100)
Source: Estimates by Bureau of Business and Economic Research, Arizona State University, Tempe, Arizona, July, 1978.

Table 10: Activity index of Arizona

Fesenmaier and Lieber (1988) also discussed the destination diversification (the set of possible relationships between the number of destinations and the number of activities in which a household might participate) through a graphic (see Figure 4). Line A in the graphic is a one-to-one relationship when each activity is considered entirely destination dependent in that each activity is perceived as totally antagonistic to all others. Line B represents the compatibility between activities, which results in a decrease in the number of destinations relative to the number of activities. This is presented in varying degrees by the lower triangle in Figure 4. Line C represents the ratio of the number of destinations per activity exceeding 1.0; in such instance any increase in the number of activities will result in a dramatic increase in the number of destinations visited.

In the work of Fesenmaier and Lieber (1988), they found that "the number of recreation facilities" could be regressed against "the total number of recreation activities" in which the household participated last year (R^2 = 0.43; regression coefficient = 0.71). The results indicated that residents of Oklahoma consider many of the respective activities to be "incompatible."

Therefore, Fesenmaier and Lieber (1988) again examined the impact of the respective activities, each household's socioeconomic status, and an opportunity index (independent variables) on the number of recreation facilities across the state (dependent variable) by using multiple partial regression analysis. The results of this analysis are presented in Table 11. It indicates that households' outdoor recreation participation patterns explain to a large degree the number of recreation facilities that Oklahoma households visited during the year because of the high partial regression coefficients of respective activities. The dependent variable and inde-

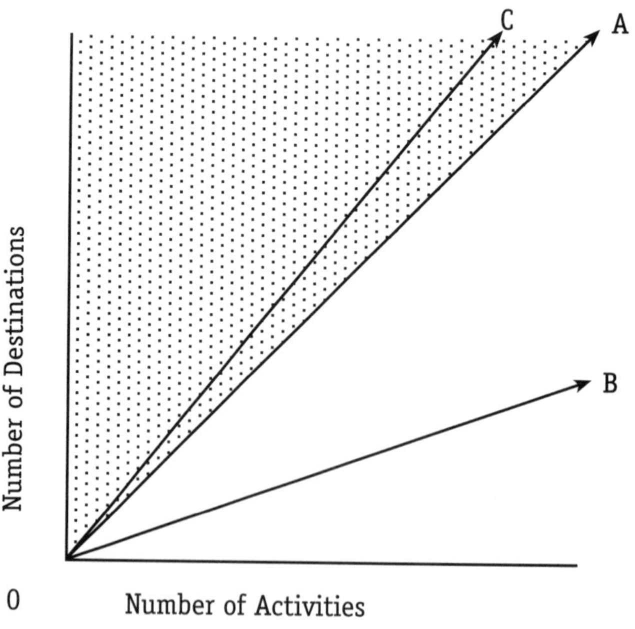

Figure 4: Hypothetical relationships between number of destinations and number of activities

Independent Variables	Partial Regression Analysis	Beta Coefficient	T Statistics•
INTERCEPT	-0.356		-0.267
RESPECTIVE ACTIVITIES			
Backpacking	0.556	0.066	2.873
Motorboating	0.509	0.185	7.103
Sailboating	0.204	0.027	1.183
Tent camping	0.323	0.096	4.045
Vehicle camping	0.334	0.099	4.279
Canoeing	1.095	0.230	10.029
Day hiking	0.467	0.111	4.807
Fishing	0.601	0.204	8.595
Hunting	0.736	0.258	11.030
Four-wheel/Off road touring	0.704	0.163	7.099
Waterskiing	0.182	0.056	2.076
Visiting a state park	0.760	0.280	12.014
HOUSEHOLDS' SOCIOECONOMIC STATUS			
Age of male household head	0.000	0.002	0.030
Age of female household head	0.002	0.020	0.287
Total number of children at home	0.015	0.015	0.588
Race of household (white/nonwhite)	-0.070	-0.014	-0.640
Residence (years) in same city/town	-0.001	-0.016	-0.600
Days of paid vacation per year	-0.003	-0.021	-0.902
Year of education	0.010	0.022	0.897
Total family income below $15,000 (y/n)	0.084	0.026	0.967
Total family income $15,000–$30,000 (y/n)	0.154	0.055	2.191
OPPORTUNITY INDEX			
No. of public facilities (0–25 miles)	-0.020	0.017	-0.434
No. of public facilities (26–50 miles)	0.033	0.051	0.777
No. of public facilities (51–75 miles)	-0.010	-0.016	-0.236
No. of public facilities (76–100 miles)	0.032	0.082	0.858
No. of public facilities (101–150 miles)	0.040	0.112	1.078
No. of public facilities (151–200 miles)	0.010	0.033	0.261
No. of public facilities (201–250 miles)	0.024	0.039	0.643
No. of public facilities (251 miles or more)	0.002	0.002	0.026

*Multiple adjusted $R^2 = 0.495$ with F value = 36.32 (Prob > F = .0001).
•Underlined values are significant at 0.005 level.
Source: Fesenmaier and Lieber, 1988

Table 11: Regression analysis of household diversification behavior

pendent variables in this partial multiple regression analysis (Table 11) are as follows:

dependent variable— the number of recreation facilities across the state (Oklahoma)

independent variables—
1. Respective activities (12 different activities)
2. Households' socioeconomic status (9 demographic variables)
3. Opportunity index (8 different variables)

Furthermore, Fesenmaier and Lieber (1988) examined the activity compatibility by developing an activity matrix and analyzing their partial regression coefficients. The results are presented in Table 12, and the entries in the "diagonal" are partial regressions for each specific activity. These may be interpreted as an index describing the degree to which an activity tends to occur at a single facility or across a number of facilities. A coefficient greater than 1.0 for a given activity could indicate that households that participated in this activity tend to recreate at a number of facilities, whereas a coefficient less than 1.0 suggests that these households tend to limit participation in that activity to a few facilities.

The off-diagonal elements are the partial regression coefficients when members of a household participated in two different activities and provide insight into

	Act1	Act2	Act3	Act4	Act5	Act6	Act7	Act8	Act9	Act10	Act11	Act12
Act1	.87*	-.06	-.41	-.28	.31	.43	-.85*	-.32	-.37	-.03	-.58	1.54*
Act2		.86*	-.03	-.08	-.16	.67*	-.18	-.27*	.07	.42*	-.71*	-.17
Act3			1.25*	.17	.35	-.90*	-1.68*	.02	.60	-.15	-.68	-.97*
Act4				.90*	-.23	.26*	-.48*	-.21	-.13	.00	-.04	-.31*
Act5					.53*	-.02	.04	.00	.46*	.00	-.45*	-.13
Act6						.65*	.31	-.17	-.43*	-.07	.20	.62*
Act7	Overall Results						.94*	.29	-.67*	-.51*	.77*	-.28
Act8	R^2 0.6040						1.13*	-.40	-.24	-.20	-.23*	
Act9	F-value 23.98							1.14*	-.52	.16	-.06	
Act10	Prob > F 0.0001									1.15*	-.17	.07
Act11	d.f. 1211										.65*	.25
Act12	*significant at .05											1.10*

Act1 = Backpacking; Act2 = Motorboating; Act3 = Sailboating; Act4 = Tent camping; Act5 = Vehicle camping; Act6 = Canoeing; Act7 = Day hiking; Act8 = Fishing; Act9 = Hunting; Act10 = Four-wheel/Off road touring; Act11 = Waterskiing; Act12 = Visiting a state park

Source: Fesenmaier and Lieber, 1988

Table 12: Coefficients of destination diversification

the conflicting or compatible nature of the respective activities. For example, negative coefficients seem to indicate that activities are compatible because their effect upon the dependent variable is to reduce the total number of destinations which are visited when both activities (the pair represented by the coefficient) are undertaken by the household. Positive coefficients, on the other hand, suggest some kind of perceived conflict between activities because the number of destinations visited would increase when households undertake both activities during a given period of time. The dependent variable and independent variables in this partial multiple regression analysis (Table 12) are as follows:

dependent variable— the number of recreation facilities across the state (Oklahoma)

independent variables— 1. 12 variables of individual activities (diagonal)
2. 66 variables of interaction activities (off-diagonal)

Main Activity Index

The Main Activity Index was developed by Huan (1997) to monitor the importance level of various activities participated in by U.S. travel parties in Canada. The data used were collected by Statistics Canada in conducting the International Travel Survey, and the survey revealed party participation in 19 different activities. In order to express the importance level of various activities pursued, different kinds of Main Activity Indices were developed for each activity. The formula is:

$$\text{Main Activity Index (activity A)} : \frac{\text{0;1 (Participated? No/Yes)}}{\text{\# of total activities}} * 100$$

From the above formula, the total number of activities participated in by a U.S. travel party is calculated. If activity A is not participated in, the dividend in the formula is zero, and its importance level to the U.S. travel party also is zero. If activity A is undertaken, the dividend in the formula is one and its importance level to the U.S. travel party is equally shared with the other activities done in terms of percentage. So, the sum of these 19 different Main Activity Indices will be 100.

The limitation to this Main Activity Index study is that expenditure, travel length, and other important factors about the specific activity are unknown in the International Travel Survey. All the activities are treated equally, regardless of the different amounts of money and travel length the travel party spends on them. This equality could cause bias. For example, a travel party may spend one day sightseeing and three days shopping. Shopping is significantly more important only if the travel length is considered. However, from the above formula of the Main Activity Index, both the importance levels of shopping and sightseeing are the same (50/50).

In Huan's study, all the activities in which U.S. travellers participated were classified into three categories: Heritage Activities, Sports or Outdoor Activities, and Non-Heritage Activities. In this section, only the heritage activities indices will be discussed.

	Activity Index			
	Act2	Act3	Act10	Act11
1990 Jan–Mar	0.65	4.01	5.46	5.02
1990 Apr–Jun	1.67	3.11	6.34	8.09
1990 Jul–Sep	2.63	2.41	6.80	8.82
1990 Oct–Dec	1.87	8.46	5.54	6.35
1991 Jan–Mar	2.16	6.28	3.94	4.01
1991 Apr–Jun	1.26	5.25	4.89	8.07
1991 Jul–Sep	2.29	3.31	6.33	9.15
1991 Oct–Dec	1.75	10.15	3.75	7.82
1992 Jan–Mar	1.07	6.46	3.98	4.18
1992 Apr–Jun	1.53	2.84	4.21	8.19
1992 Jul–Sep	2.65	3.75	7.04	8.72
1992 Oct–Dec	1.68	8.61	3.18	6.93
1993 Jan–Mar	1.34	5.35	3.75	7.77
1993 Apr–Jun	1.17	4.73	4.30	8.55
1993 Jul–Sep	2.16	5.95	5.50	8.66
1993 Oct–Dec	1.26	11.85	4.92	7.16
1994 Jan–Mar	1.23	5.85	7.68	7.18
1994 Apr–Jun	1.44	5.23	4.08	7.09
1994 Jul–Sep	1.87	5.41	5.03	11.11
1994 Oct–Dec	2.01	10.78	3.75	6.94
1995 Jan–Mar	1.09	6.21	7.55	6.01
1995 Apr–Jun	2.44	5.96	4.54	7.36
1995 Jul–Sep	1.91	4.39	5.46	11.75
1995 Oct–Dec	2.01	9.78	3.35	6.15

Act

2. Attending festivals or fairs
3. Attending cultural events (plays, etc.)
10. Visiting a zoo, museum, or natural display
11. Visiting a national, provincial, regional park or historic site

Source: Huan, 1997

Table 13: Main activity index of U.S. Great Lakes region travellers in Ontario (Heritage activity)

In Table 13 and Figure 5, "Visiting a national, provincial, regional park or historic site" was the most important heritage activity for U.S. overnight pleasure travellers. "Visiting a zoo, museum, or natural display" was the second most popular heritage activity. The above two heritage activities were particularly important during the spring and summer seasons (from April to September). During the fall season (from October to December), "Attending cultural events" (plays, concerts, etc.) was the most important heritage activity for U.S. travellers, but was only the third most important heritage activity in other seasons (from January to September).

Tourism Barometers

The Tourism Barometer provides a measure of the relative changes in tourist activity over time. At the national level in the U.S., the Tourism Barometer was used by the U.S. Travel Data Center (USTDC). At the regional level, the Tourism Barometer was applied to examine regional activity by using different criteria (see Table 14).

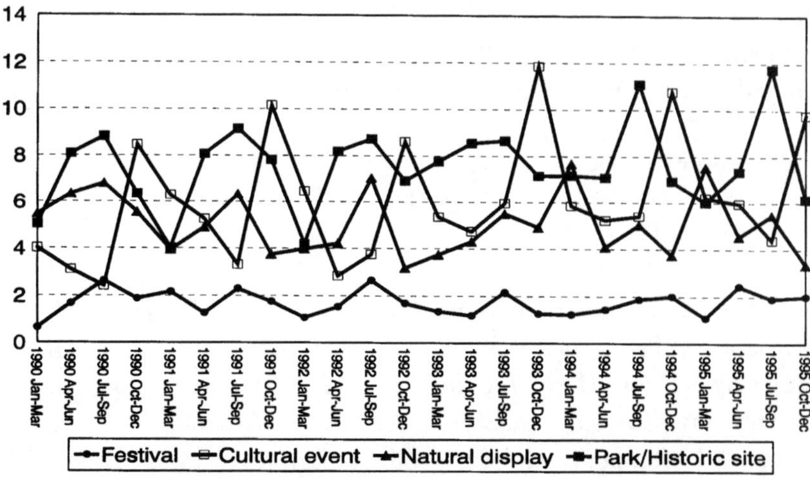

"Attending festivals or fairs" was the fourth (the least) popular heritage activity U.S. travel parties participated in Canada. The importance levels of these activities changed significantly across the different seasons. Generally speaking, the importance level of each heritage activity was low; however, the four heritage activities were still important to U.S. travellers.
Source: Huan, 1997

Figure 5: Main Activity Index of U.S. Great Lakes region travellers in Ontario (heritage activity)

City/State	The Indices	Researchers
Arizona	Arizona Tourism Barometer Arizona Tourism Barometer	Bond and McDonald, 1978 Hogan and Rex, 1984
Duluth, MN	Duluth Tourist Index Local Area Tourist Index	Cong (unpublished) Peterson (unpublished)
Kentucky	Travel Barometer	Kentucky Department of Economic Development
Mobile, AL	Composite Visitor Index	University of South Alabama
North Carolina	N. Carolina Travel Index Lodging Index	Judd and Rulison, 1983 Wassenaar and Stafford, 1991
Texas	Tourism Index Tourism Activity Index	Backman and Uysal, 1987 Vina, Hollas, Merrifield, and Ford, 1994
Virginia	Virginia Travel Barometer	Virginia Department of Economic Development
Williamsburg, VA	Williamsburg Business	Bureau of Business Research, College of William and Mary

Source: Vina, Hollas, Merrifield, and Ford, 1994

Table 14: Tourism Barometer at the regional level

The Arizona Tourism Barometer, which was developed by Bond and McDonald (1978) and employed only activity levels (attendance), is called an *Activity Index* by Backman and Uysal (1992). The formula for this Arizona Tourism Barometer is:

$$I = \sum_{L=1}^{n} \frac{\text{Activity (L, QTR)}}{\text{Activity (L, Base)/4}} * \text{Weight (L)}$$

The base year is 1976.

Another Arizona Tourism Barometer was developed by Hogan and Rex (1984). The information utilized in this index is (1) length of stay in the state, (2) trip expenditures by category (food, lodging, etc.), and (3) where the people went and how long they stayed in each place while they visited Arizona.

The North Carolina Travel Index (Tourism Barometer) was developed by Judd and Rulison (1983). Before developing the index, the monthly gross retail sales by hotels and motels in North Carolina were adjusted by using (1) the Consumer Price Index for urban areas and (2) month-to-month seasonal variation. The monthly price-adjusted sales were then compared to the average level of sales for 1975 (= 100). The sample calculation for the North Carolina Travel Index is:

1. Hotels and motels, current

Gross monthly sales ($1,000) January 1981 = $23,971

2. Consumer Price Index—Urban January 1981 = 260.5

3. Calculate sales adjusted for price level:

Adjusted sales = 100 x (current sales/CPI-U)
= 100 x ($23,971/260.5)
= $9,201.9

4. Calculate travel index:

Crude index = 100 x (adjusted sales/index base)
= 100 x (9,201.9/10,200)
= 90.2

5. Calculate seasonally adjusted travel index:

Seasonally adjusted index
= 100 x (crude N.C. travel index/seasonal factor)
= 100 x (90.2/69.5)
= 129.8

Vina, Hollas, Merrifield, and Ford (1994) developed a principal components-based Tourism Activity Index (Tourism Barometer) for Texas. The variables which comprised the San Antonio Tourism Activity Index include (1) state hotel tax collections from San Antonio, adjusted for the change in the tax rate and also deflated for inflation using the average price of a hotel room in the city (TAX) (information obtained from the Texas State Comptroller of Public Accounts), (2) hotel room nights sold in San Antonio (HT) (information obtained from the Source Strategies Inc.), (3) deplanements at the San Antonio International Airport (AIR) (information obtained from the City of San Antonio Aviation Department), and (4) attendance at San Antonio tourist attractions (ATT) (information obtained from the figure provided directly by attractions). The formula for the index developed by Vina, Hollas, Merrifield, and Ford (1994) is:

$$TOURISM = a(TAX) + b(HT) + c(AIR) + d(ATT) + U_{TOURISM}$$

where $U_{TOURISM}$ is error term.
These variables were chosen based on both the quality of the data and necessary historic time series. Then, these variables were standardized. The base year chosen is 1989. The average of the four quarters of 1989 is standardized as 100.

Each activity sample stratum is weighted according to its relative quantity in the base year. Comparison of the current quarter with the average quarter in the base year produces a value that includes seasonal variation, an important component of tourist activity levels (Bond and McDonald, 1978). Moreover, Shishkin's seasonality factors could be employed to deseasonalize the activity levels for the current quarter to generate a seasonally adjusted index value. This seasonal adjustment was carried out using the X-11 seasonal adjustment program developed by the U.S. Department of Commerce and available for use with the SAS system (SAS Institute, 1980).

Travel Frequency

Schmidhauser (1975) discusses the concept of travel frequency, which refers to the average number of trips taken by a person participating in tourism in a given period. The Travel Frequency can be estimated by the following formula:

$$Tf = \frac{T_p}{p} = \frac{GTP}{NTP}$$

where T_p is the total number of trips undertaken by the population in question,
p is the number of persons in a particular population group who have made at least one trip away from home in a given period.

Trip Index

Trip Indices are used to measure travel time. The Trip Indices relate the length of stay in a country or at a destination to the total length of trip (Pearce and Elliot, 1983; Uysal and McDonald, 1989). The formula is:

$$TI = \frac{D_n}{T_n} * 100$$

where D_n is nights spent at destination
T_n is total nights spent on the trip

When the Trip Index is 100, the entire trip is spent at the one destination. If the index is 10, the destination would account for only 10% of the total trip length. As the index is 0, it means that no overnight stay is made in the study area. The higher the Trip Index of a destination, the more important the destination is.

Pearce and Elliott (1983) introduced a relative measure of travel time, the Trip Index, and illustrated its use with reference to two empirical studies from New Zealand. The Trip Index related the nights spent at a destination to the total length of the trip or holiday. In Table 15, the Trip Indices of Westland National Park and Christchurch were detailed. For the Westland National Park tourists, around 20% of them were same day visitors; most tourists (92.6%) spent less than 20% of their trip length at Westland National Park. For the Christchurch tourists, almost all (98%) of them were overnight visitors; half (50%) of the Christchurch tourists spent less than 20% of their trip length at Christchurch. However, there were about one-fifth (17%) of the Christchurch tourists who chose it as their only destination. Generally speaking, both Westland National Park and Christchurch were stopover destinations.

Trip Index	Westland National Park (N = 1028)	Christchurch (N = 756)
0	20.8%	2%
1-10	55.5	23
11-20	16.3	25
21-50	4.5	21
51-99	0.7	9
100	2.2	17
not stated	-	3

Source: Pearce and Elliott, 1983

Table 15: Trip Index by Pearce and Elliott

Uysal and McDonald (1989) applied the idea of a Trip Index in studying the relative importance of city destinations in South Carolina (see Table 16). Three segmentations based on Trip Index (I, Low, 1–30; II, Medium, 31–60; III, High, 61-100) were developed. The two coastal city destinations (Hilton Head and Myrtle Beach) are located in the upper level of the Trip Index, suggesting that a significant number of visitors make these cities their principal destination (Trip Index 61–100).

Furthermore, nearly one-half of Segment III (41%) listed the two cities as their sole destinations. More vacation time is being spent by many of these visitors in the coastal area. On the other hand, Greenville, and to a lesser extent Columbia, appear to be important as stopovers and/or short trip destinations. While traditional length-of-stay data do give some indication of the nature of visits to the area, the Trip Index provides a broader perspective and reveals more information regarding the relative importance of each destination within the state context.

	Destination					
	Myrtle Beach	Charleston	Hilton Head	Columbia	Green-ville	Others
I: Low (1–30)	18.5	46.4	10.7	36.0	50.0	34.4
II: Medium (31–60)	24.1	28.6	35.7	32.0	33.3	24.7
III: High (61–100)	57.4	25.0	53.6	32.0	16.7	40.9
Average nights spent	6.2	3.3	7.3	3.4	2.4	4.7

Source: Uysal and McDonald, 1989

Table 16: Trip Index by Uysal and McDonald

Oppermann (1992a, 1993) extended the application of the Trip Index to 30 destinations in New Zealand and also applied it to destination throughout Malaysia. Most New Zealand destinations recorded values below 10, indicative of their stopover function. Results from Malaysia were much higher, attaining values of up to 100 in the case of the Club Mediterranée resort and over 60 for Penang and the hill resort in the Genting Highlands.

Murphy (1992) incorporated seasonal variations in his application of the Trip Index to Vancouver Island, British Columbia, and was able to develop a functional classification of the area and identify a hierarchical spatial pattern influenced by the location of the island's two principal gateways.

Huan (1997) also utilized a Trip Index to measure and monitor the importance level of destinations visited by U.S. Great Lakes region overnight pleasure travel parties in Ontario, Canada. The Trip Index formula for the Ontario regions (OTAPs) is:

$$\text{Trip Index (OTAP 1/12):} \quad \frac{\text{Total nights in OTAP 1/12}}{\text{Total nights in Canada}} * 100$$

From the above formula, it can be seen that the Trip Index indicates the importance levels of a travel region for a U.S. travel party, in comparison with their travel length to other Ontario regions. In Tables 17, 18 and Figures 6, 7, Ontario South is shown to be more important than Ontario North.

Moreover, Metro Toronto (OTAP 4) was the major destination for U.S. travellers and it was more important than any other Ontario region (OTAPs), especially in the fall season (from October to December). The second major destination in Ontario South was Festival Country (OTAP 2). Since 1992, there has been no significant seasonal change in its level of importance. Southwestern Ontario (OTAP 1) was the third major destination in Ontario South.

As for the other Ontario South regions, their importance levels were almost the same as the Ontario North regions. For the Ontario North regions, their im-

	Trip Index of OTAPs					
	1	2	3	4	5	6
1990 Jan–Mar	14.09	24.34	2.82	34.40	1.76	3.10
1990 Apr–Jun	11.88	20.54	1.53	23.00	3.97	15.00
1990 Jul-Sep	12.01	30.33	2.89	19.15	1.80	8.80
1990 Oct–Dec	14.28	24.59	1.29	35.69	1.08	5.65
1991 Jan–Mar	18.46	15.27	2.04	33.23	2.03	4.29
1991 Apr–Jun	12.91	18.66	1.05	21.98	6.96	10.29
1991 Jul-Sep	12.44	18.79	2.62	20.99	1.94	7.73
1991 Oct–Dec	12.35	20.92	1.41	41.97	1.45	4.22
1992 Jan–Mar	19.50	29.95	0.22	32.78	0.19	3.77
1992 Apr–Jun	7.72	30.45	1.72	24.75	3.71	6.08
1992 Jul-Sep	12.83	22.20	2.49	21.34	3.00	9.17
1992 Oct–Dec	14.97	23.75	1.62	39.08	2.55	4.12
1993 Jan–Mar	10.80	23.16	5.15	35.07	0.96	4.54
1993 Apr–Jun	10.01	21.67	2.03	21.02	3.00	7.72
1993 Jul-Sep	9.63	21.35	4.81	24.23	4.96	8.92
1993 Oct–Dec	8.86	21.99	1.95	37.69	2.51	3.88
1994 Jan–Mar	10.96	22.92	2.50	35.17	4.49	5.39
1994 Apr–Jun	9.07	20.46	3.41	26.56	2.34	10.09
1994 Jul-Sep	13.93	22.25	4.06	17.60	5.01	9.62
1994 Oct–Dec	15.41	27.15	0.38	41.99	1.26	2.30
1995 Jan–Mar	11.30	20.24	1.90	34.18	4.07	5.95
1995 Apr–Jun	10.62	23.24	2.96	22.10	2.22	10.18
1995 Jul-Sep	13.93	21.70	3.36	16.55	3.19	9.02
1995 Oct–Dec	15.25	23.51	0.92	36.76	1.17	5.94

OTAPs

1. Southwestern Ontario
2. Festival Country
3. Georgian Highland
4. Metro Toronto
5. Central
6. Eastern

Source: Huan, 1997

Table 17: Trip Index of U.S. Great Lakes region travellers in Ontario (Ontario South)

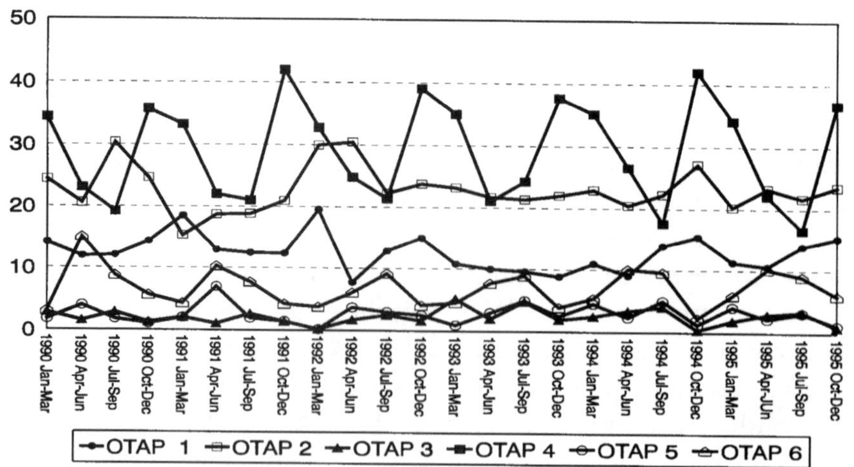

Source: Huan, 1997

Figure 6: Trip Index of U.S. Great Lakes region travellers in Ontario (Ontario South)

	Trip Index of OTAPs					
	7	8	9	10	11	12
1990 Jan-Mar	1.05	1.03	10.59	0.06	2.23	1.52
1990 Apr-Jun	0.59	0.96	3.48	0.71	2.60	8.49
1990 Jul-Sep	1.00	3.40	3.48	0.41	2.20	3.56
1990 Oct-Dec	0.04	0.19	5.85	0.00	0.93	2.81
1991 Jan-Mar	0.06	0.18	8.72	0.02	0.92	3.19
1991 Apr-Jun	2.24	0.81	1.84	0.48	4.02	8.61
1991 Jul-Sep	1.79	2.19	3.74	0.07	6.98	4.46
1991 Oct-Dec	0.03	1.37	5.51	0.09	1.52	2.84
1992 Jan-Mar	0.00	0.00	6.36	0.00	0.79	1.77
1992 Apr-Jun	0.46	0.70	2.00	0.53	3.38	8.42
1992 Jul-Sep	0.78	2.18	3.26	0.78	4.80	4.58
1992 Oct-Dec	0.00	0.99	5.50	0.08	0.41	1.68
1993 Jan-Mar	0.00	0.00	8.18	0.00	1.46	1.70
1993 Apr-Jun	0.42	1.13	6.99	0.24	3.04	8.00
1993 Jul-Sep	0.76	1.80	3.49	0.48	4.27	5.25
1993 Oct-Dec	0.00	0.84	12.45	0.00	0.76	0.74
1994 Jan-Mar	0.00	1.11	7.61	0.00	1.19	1.28
1994 Apr-Jun	0.67	1.14	6.09	0.19	2.75	4.29
1994 Jul-Sep	1.76	1.72	4.40	0.49	3.64	3.46
1994 Oct-Dec	0.00	0.23	1.49	0.00	0.19	2.16
1995 Jan-Mar	1.26	0.95	7.59	0.00	3.44	1.87
1995 Apr-Jun	0.44	0.74	2.38	0.26	3.22	5.71
1995 Jul-Sep	1.22	1.35	4.94	0.69	5.04	7.04
1995 Oct-Dec	0.00	0.12	3.14	0.00	0.82	1.25

OTAPs

7. Algonquin-Nippissing
8. Rainbow Country
9. Algoma-Kinniwabi
10. Cochrane-Timiskaming
11. North of Superior
12. North-western

Source: Huan, 1997

Table 18: Trip Index of U.S. Great Lakes region travellers in Ontario (Ontario North)

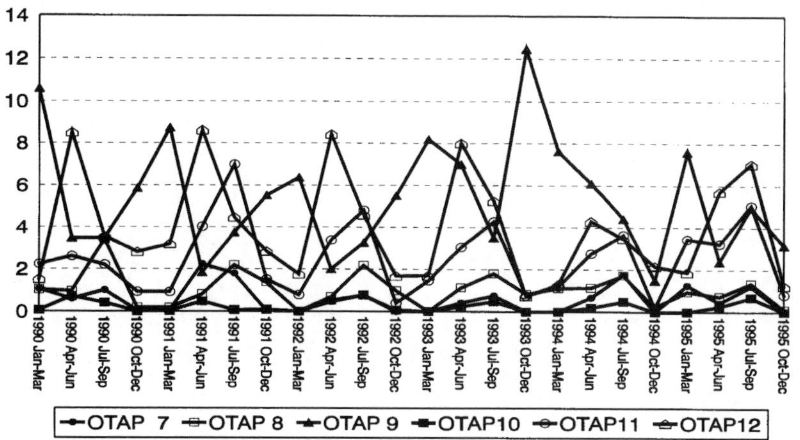

Source: Huan, 1997

Figure 7: Trip Index of U.S. Great Lakes region travellers in Ontario (Ontario North)

portance levels to a U.S. travel party were low. Most U.S. travellers did not spend more than 10% of their trip length in individual Ontario North regions. Generally speaking, the Algoma–Kinniwabi (OTAP 9) and Northwestern (OTAP 12) regions were the major Ontario North destinations.

The third major destination, North of Superior (OTAP 11), was more important than Algonquin–Nippissing (OTAP 7), Rainbow Country (OTAP 8), and Cochrane–Timiskaming (OTAP 10). Although the Trip Indices of all Ontario North regions were very small, the overall Ontario North area as a consolidated region can also be treated as an important destination.

Clough (1987) pointed out two problems with using the Trip Index. An obvious problem is that visits other than overnight stays are discounted. The decision to stay overnight at a given location may have little to do with the attraction of that location; rather, it may reflect such factors as availability of accommodation, stage of journey, or weather and traffic conditions encountered at the time. A second problem with the Trip Index is that if a destination's relative importance is reflected in the "time accorded to visit it," the formulation ignores the time taken to travel to the destination. There are locations which people value highly enough to travel out of their way to visit, but where they don't stay. The Trip Index was modified by Clough (1987) in the following way:

$$TI^* = [D_t/(T_n+1)24]\times 100$$

where Dt = time at destination measured in hours,
Tn = is total nights spent on the trip.

Having first developed the Trip Index, Pearce (1987) replied to the above problems identified by Clough noting that the distinction between a day or transit visit and an overnight stay is critical for many aspects of tourism research and planning. Expenditures on accommodation can often account for up to half of a visitor's daily expenditure, and the location of overnight stops markedly influences the pattern of economic impact.

4

Geographical/Population Indices

THIS CHAPTER ADDRESSES Geographical/Population Indices. By comparing the visitor population from different countries or political regions, the travel organizations can understand the importance of their different tourism market segments and better promote their target markets. In this group, the Brand Development Index (BDI) has been employed as a decision tool for allocating advertising expenditures and is calculated as the ratio of brand sales to population (Sissors and Surmanek, 1982). The Category Development Index (CDI) is similar to the BDI except that it is based on the percentage of sales of a product category in a given market rather than a brand (Sissors and Surmanek, 1982). The Compactness Index is one measure which describes the shape of the area. The shape is a simple and valid measure of the overall internal accessibility of the region—the more compact the region, the easier it will be to ship commodities or to move tourists around, *ceteris paribus* (Smith, 1995).

The Connectivity Index describes the overall accessibility of a region in terms of the level of interconnectivity among nodes in the network (Smith, 1995). The Country Potential Generation Index/Region Potential Generation Index (CPGI/RPGI) has been used to assess the relative capacity of a country/region to generate trips (Hudman, 1979, 1980). The Destination Perception Index was developed to measure college students' perception of world regions as tourism destinations (Rafferty, 1990).

The Directional Bias Index is a simple measure of the vacation travel tendency for one particular direction (Wolfe, 1966). Gross Travel Propensity is the other type of travel propensity developed by Schmidhauser (1975, 1976) and it is analogous to the concept of "trip per capita," which also expresses trips as a ratio of the total population of the region in question (Van Doren and Stubbles, 1975). The Main Destination Ratio is developed to analyze flows of travellers and tourists (Leiper, 1989).

Net Travel Propensity refers to the proportion of the total population or a particular group in the population who have made at least one trip away from home in the period of question (usually a year) (Schmidhauser, 1975, 1976). The Recreation Index was developed by Gardavsky (1977) to monitor weekend recreation in Czechoslovakia involving staying at private chalets or cottages (second homes). It is calculated by dividing the potential recreation area by the number of second homes. The Relative Acceptance Index measures the relative success of a destination in attracting tourists from a generating country (Williams and Zelinsky, 1970).

The Tourism Location Score was developed by Fridgen (1983, 1987) to compare tourism locations and counties in an attempt to provide a straightforward method of qualifying the data obtained from cognitive maps. The Travel Propensity Index is an extension of the CPGI Index, which was created by simply dividing the CPGI index by the per capita income of the respective country (Hudman, 1979): the higher the Travel Propensity Index is, the higher the degree of mobility (potential ability to travel). All the original ideas, technical formula, statistical outputs, and applications of the indices in this Geographical/Population Indices group will be detailed in the following part of this section.

Brand Development Index

The Brand Development Index (BDI) has been employed as a decision tool for allocating advertising expenditures (Sissors and Surmanek, 1982). It is calculated as the ratio of brand sales (e.g., Harley-Davidson sales versus all motorcycle sales) to population. If a region has 6% of the U.S. population but only 2% own Harley-Davidsons, it would appear that the brand is not well developed in that region and the Brand Development Index is low. On the contrary, if the Brand Development Index is high, it means that the brand is well developed. In a word, the BDI is an index number representing sales potential. The larger the sales in a market relative to population percentage, the higher the BDI in that market. The original BDI formula by Sissors and Surmanek (1982) is as follows:

$$\text{BDI} = \frac{\text{\% of a brand's total U.S. sales in Market X}}{\text{\% of total U.S. population in Market X}} * 100$$

Bonn and Brand (1995) applied this technique in travel and tourism for Tampa, Florida. The formula for the Brand Development Index was modified as follows:

$$\text{BDI} = \frac{\text{Tvisit}}{\text{Population}} * 100$$

where BDI = Brand Development Index
Tvisit = percentage of visitors to Tampa, Florida
Population = percentage of U.S. population in market.

From the above formula, Bonn and Brand (1995) developed a series of Brand Development Indices (Table 19) and used them to generate an opportunity matrix (Table 20) for Tampa, Florida. The tourism opportunity matrix depicted Top Performers, Sleeping Giants, Untapped Potential, and Low Priorities. Each category represents pleasure travel markets corresponding to the quadrants of the matrix: High Population/High BDI, Low Population/High BDI, High Population/Low BDI, Low Population/Low BDI. By this opportunity matrix, different market strategies can be developed for specific market segments.

The Brand Development Index is a marketing tool that has traditionally been used to identify market potential for goods and products. In Bonn and Brand's (1995) work, it was found to be a very successful tool, particularly when combined with the opportunity matrix. BDI has tremendous potential for destinations, attractions, and other hospitality services.

Category Development Index

The Category Development Index (CDI) is similar to the BDI except that it is based on the percentage of sales of a product category in a given market rather than a brand. The method of calculating the CDI (Sissors and Surmanek, 1982) is as follows:

1992 Tampa, Florida, Visitation/BDI Report Pleasure Market					
ADI— Area of Dominant Influence	# of ADI Households (1,000s)	% of U.S. Households Excluding FL	% of Florida Visitors	% of Tampa Visitors	Tampa/ BDI
Grand Rapids/Kalamazoo, MI	6112.7	0.71%	0.7%	1.6%	225
St. Louis, MO	1110.9	1.30	1.4	2.2	169
Pittsburgh, PA	1139.6	1.30	1.4	2.1	161
Cincinnati, OH	759.0	0.88	1.1	1.5	136
Chicago, IL	2999.7	3.50	3.6	4.5	129
Detroit, MI	1719.0	1.99	1.7	2.4	121
Richmond, VA	436.9	0.50	0.4	0.6	120
Louisville/Lexington, KY	891.9	1.04	1.3	1.2	115
Atlanta, GA	1456.8	1.70	6.0	1.9	112
Buffalo, NY	629.4	0.73	0.7	0.8	110
Harrisburg, PA	42.9	0.63	0.7	0.6	95
Washington, DC	1781.1	2.10	2.6	1.9	90
Raleigh-Durham, NC	729.3	0.84	0.9	0.7	83
Baton Rouge, LA	249.5	0.79	0.4	0.1	34
Springfield, MA	247.7	0.29	0.3	0.1	34
Jackson, MS	276.1	0.32	0.5	0.1	31

Source: Bonn and Brand, 1995

Table 19: BDI calculation for the representative city of Tampa

Untapped Potentials BDI: 70–99		Untapped Potentials BDI: 70–99	
Harrisburg, PA	95	Grand Rapids, MI	225
Washington, DC	90	Cincinnati, OH	170
Raleigh, NC	83	St. Louis, MO	169
		Pittsburgh, PA	161
		Chicago, IL	129
		Detroit, MI	121
Untapped Potentials BDI: 70–99		**Untapped Potentials BDI: 70–99**	
Baton Rouge, LA	34	Richmond, VA	120
Springfield, MA	34	Louisville, KY	115
Jackson, MS	31	Atlanta, GA	112
		Providence, RI	110

Source: Bonn and Brand, 1995

Table 20: Opportunity matrix for Tampa, Florida

$$\text{BDI} = \frac{\text{\% of a product category's total U.S. sales in Market X}}{\text{\% of total U.S. population in Market X}} * 100$$

Both the BDI and CDI are useful in decision making. One tells the planner the relative strengths and weaknesses for the brand and the other, the relative strengths and weaknesses for the category. Further, Sissors and Surmanek (1982) suggested that planners use the BDI-CDI data for each market in decision making. The BDI/CDI relationships of the market are presented in Table 21. The possible results are presented and detailed in the following.

1. High BDI and high CDI.
   This kind of market usually represents good sales potential for both the brand and the category.

2. High BDI and low CDI.
   Here the category is not selling well, but the brand is. Probably a good market in which to advertise, but surely one to watch to see if the brand's sales decline over time.

3. Low BDI and high CDI.
   This kind of market shows potential for the category but demands that someone study the reason why the brand is not doing well here. Is it because of poor distribution? Not enough advertising dollars, GRPs, or reach in the market? To advertise in this market without knowing the answer would be a risk.

	High BDI	Low BDI
High CDI	High share of market Good market potential	Low share of market Good market potential
Low CDI	High share of market Monitor for sales decline	Low share of market Poor market potential

Source: Sissors and Surmanek, 1982

Table 21: BDI/CDI relationships

4. Low BDI and low CDI.
   This kind of market represents a risk for any brand. Here, too, a planner might want to know why the category doesn't sell well. Such a market would probably not be a good place to advertise under most circumstances.

Bonn and Brand (1995) also pointed out that in the traditional products application, a Category Development Index is computed by first identifying market territories or regions, then further defining each territory or region by its percent of total U.S. population, by its percent of total U.S. households, or by similar comparisons based at any number of microlevels, such as cities or destination areas. The CDI then becomes the ratio of consumption intensity (sales) to population.

Bonn and Brand (1995) applied this technique in travel and tourism industry for Tampa, Florida, and the results are presented in Table 22. The formula for the Category Development Index was modified as follows:

$$CDI = \frac{Visit}{Population} * 100$$

where *CDI*= Category Development Index
Visit = percentage of visitors to Florida
Population = percentage of U.S. population in market.

Compactness Index

The Compactness Index is one of the indices which describe the shape of the area. Shape is a simple and valid measure of the overall internal accessibility of the region (Smith, 1995). The more compact the region, the easier it will be to ship commodities or to move tourists around, *ceteris paribus*.

A number of shape indices have been developed by geographers and an overview of these was described by Coffey (1981). One of the measures depicted by Coffey is the Compactness Index—C. Smith (1995) declares that the use of C is appropriate because of the emphasis placed by planners on providing services to tourists in a region. The difficulties of service provision tend to vary inversely with a region's compactness. The measure is also useful as an indicator of the relative

1992 Tampa, Florida, Visitation/BDI Report Pleasure Market					
ADI— Area of Dominant Influence	# of ADI Households (1,000s)	% of U.S. Households Excluding FL	% of Florida Visitors	% of Tampa Visitors	Florida/ CDI
Grand Rapids/Kalamazoo, MI	6112.7	0.71%	0.7%	1.6%	113
St. Louis, MO	1110.9	1.30	1.4	2.2	108
Pittsburgh, PA	1139.6	1.30	1.4	2.1	108
Cincinnati, OH	759.0	0.88	1.1	1.5	125
Chicago, IL	2999.7	3.5	3.6	4.5	103
Detroit, MI	1719.0	1.99	1.7	2.4	85
Richmond, VA	436.9	0.50	0.4	0.6	80
Louisville/Lexington, KY	891.9	1.04	1.3	1.2	125
Atlanta, GA	1456.8	1.70	6.0	1.9	353
Buffalo, NY	629.4	0.73	0.7	0.8	96
Harrisburg, PA	42.9	0.63	0.7	0.6	111
Washington, DC	1781.1	2.1	2.6	1.9	124
Raleigh-Durham, NC	729.3	0.84	0.9	0.7	107
Baton Rouge, LA	249.5	0.79	0.4	0.1	138
Springfield, MA	247.7	0.29	0.3	0.1	103
Jackson, MS	276.1	0.32	0.5	0.1	156

Source: Bonn and Brand, 1995

Table 22: CDI calculation for representative city of Tampa

degree of physical contact with surrounding regions (potential origins or destinations). The less compact the shape, the greater the relative boundary length and the greater the degree of contact with adjacent regions. On the contrary, the more compact a region, the easier it will be to ship commodities or to move tourists around.

The reference formula of the above Compactness Index described by Coffey (1981) is as follows:

$$C = \frac{D}{D'}$$

where D is $2\sqrt{(A/)\pi}$, and A designates the area of the region,
D' is the greatest diagonal of the region.

The reason why D is $2\sqrt{(A/)\pi}$ is that the area of a circle can be obtained by the mathematical formula, $A = \pi * (D/2)^2$. For a certain area, the most compact shape is a circle with the shortest diagonal ($D = 2\sqrt{(A/)\pi}$). If its greatest diagonal is much longer than D, the extreme value of C is 0.00 and the region would be a line (the least compact). If its greatest diagonal is very close to D, the extreme value of C is 1.00 and the region would be a circle (the most compact). The higher the value of

C, the more compact the region. More compact regions have a greater degree of internal accessibility.

Smith (1995) presented two countries, Zimbabwe and Chile, as examples (see Figure 8). The area of Chile from the map is 56 square units with the greatest diagonal 40 units. The Compactness Index of Chile is 0.21 ($C=D/D'=8.44/40=0.21$ where $D = 2\sqrt{(A/)\pi} = 2\sqrt{[56/3.1416]}8.44$). So, Chile is not very compact, since it is an elongated country. The area of Zimbabwe from the map is 234 square units with the greatest diagonal 21 units. The Compactness Index of Zimbabwe is 0.82 ($C = D/D' = 17.26/21 = 0.82$ where $D = 2\sqrt{(A/)\pi} = 2\sqrt{[234/3.1416]}=17.26$). Zimbabwe is determined to be a compact country.

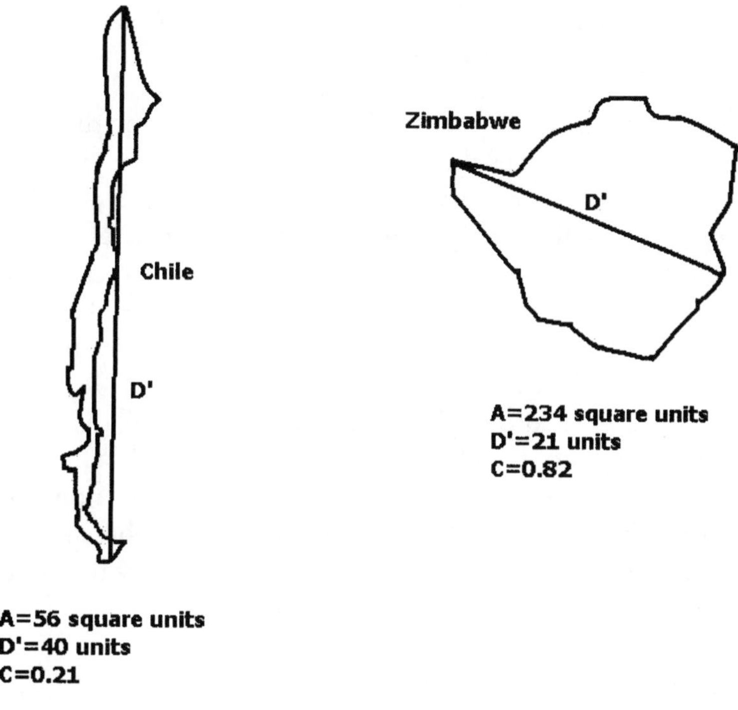

Source: Smith, 1995

Figure 8: Indices of compactness

Connectivity Index

The Connectivity Index describes the overall accessibility of a region in terms of the level of interconnectivity among nodes in the network (Smith, 1995). The measure of accessibility with reference to tourism is based on the fact that travel generally follows established routes and these routes, links connecting origin and destination nodes, form a transportation network. In general, the higher the level of connectivity, the better for tourism.

The Connectivity Index comes from a branch of mathematics known as *graph theory*, which is concerned with the properties of networks. Taylor (1977) examines six basic measures used by graph theorists. The gamma index, *r*, which is one of the six measures and is also called relative connectivity index, is the most useful for tourism. The formula is as follows:

$$r = \frac{L}{3(P-2)} = \frac{\text{Actual links}}{\text{Possible links}}$$ good only for planar network (road/rail linkages)

or

$$r = \frac{L}{(0.5)p(P-1)} = \frac{\text{Actual links}}{\text{Possible links}}$$ good only for non-planar network (the flight paths of airlines)

where L is the number of direct (actual) links between pairs of points,
P is the number of points.

From the above formula, the gamma index, *r*, is based on the ratio of actual to possible linkages. The higher the degree of connectivity, the higher the value. A value of zero (0) means that a system of points is unconnected; one (1) means that a system of points is all directly connected. The weakness of the gamma index (Connectivity Index) is that it indicates nothing about the ease of travel, travel time, or the lengths of individual line segments. For example, if an area is enlarged by 10 times, the Connectivity Index is still the same. However, the accessibility of the original area and the enlarged area are different.

Smith (1995) used a Swedish road network to develop a Connectivity Index (see Figure 9). The value of 0.52 indicates a system with only a moderate degree of connectivity. While the Swedish road network is changed to a non-planar network such as flight paths of airlines, the value is reduced to 0.25 because there are more possible linkages if we are free to "hop" over established lines to connect all points on the network.

Country/Region Potential Generation Index (CPGI/RPGI)

The CPGI/RPGI has been used to assess the relative capacity of a country/ region to generate trips (Hudman, 1979, 1980). For example, to obtain the RPGI, there are three steps involved. First, the number of trips generated by a region is divided by the total number of trips taken through the country in a given time period. This part of the index indicates the ability of each region to produce trips. Secondly, the region's population is divided by the population of the country. The result of the second step describes the relative position of the region in relation to the country's population.

Finally, the quotient of the first step is divided by the second step to get the Region Potential Generation Index. An index of 1.0 indicates an average generation capacity, while an index of less than 1.0 shows that the region generates fewer trips than its population would suggest. In contrast, an index greater than 1.0 indicates that the region generates more trips than its population would suggest. The Potential Generation Index is useful to show travel flows and demands in space

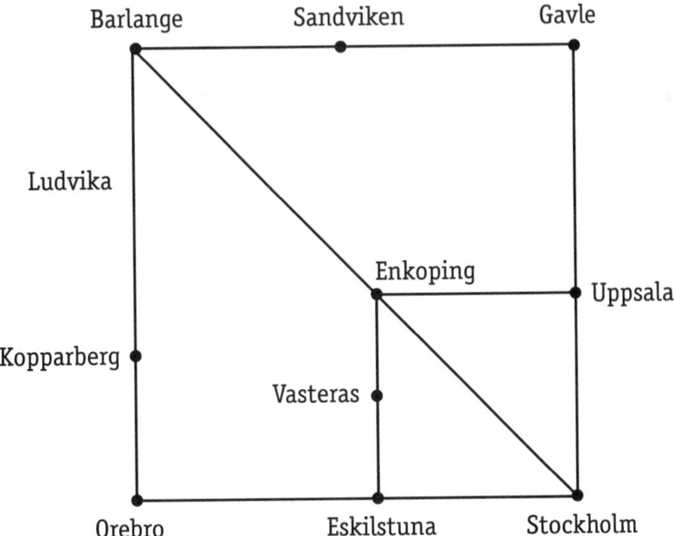

Source: Smith, 1995

Figure 9: Index of linkage connectivity: a Swedish road network

based on the number of trips and population. In addition, it reveals the relative importance of propensity to generate trips and provides the opportunity to review travel activity between regions.

The results of the CPGI developed by Hudman (1979) are presented in Table 23 and its formula is as follows.

$$\text{CPGI} = \frac{N_R/N_C}{P_R/P_C}$$

where N_R is the number of trips generated by the region
N_C is the number of trips generated in the country
P_R is the population of the region
P_C is the population of the country

McDougall (1986) also has applied the idea of RPGI to develop a travel intensity index to study the travel flow of Canadian travellers. The Canadian Travellers were segmented into four groups by their travel destinations (Canada, United States, other countries, and non-travellers). The index was developed by the socio-demographic characteristics in term of age, marital status, education, income, occupation, and geographic origin for each segment (see Table 24). For Canadians travelling to domestic destinations, a person between the ages of 25–34 with an index of 113 was more inclined to go on a domestic trip than those in any other age bracket.

There is a high correlation between a person's level of education and his or her likelihood to travel. This is reflected by the steady rise in the intensity index with increases in educational attainment. For Canadians travelling to the United States,

Country	CPGI	Country	CPGI
1. Germany, Fed Rep.	11.88	29. Spain	1.37
2. German Dem. Rep.	11.69	30. Norway	1.30
3. Switzerland	10.12	31. Greece	.95
4. Netherlands	9.71	32. Turkey	.81
5. Canada	8.01	33. Malaysia	.80
6. Luxembourg	8.00	34. Lebanon	.71
7. Portugal	7.60	35. Mexico	.62
8. Denmark	7.38	36. Argentina	.62
9. Belgium	7.24	37. Japan	.51
10. Austria	6.47	38. Saudi Arabia	.47
11. Czechoslovakia	6.12	39. Romania	.42
12. Hungary	5.92	40. Venezuela	.36
13. Poland	5.68	41. Iraq	.29
14. Ireland, Rep.	5.42	42. Chile	.19
15. France	5.20	43. Egypt	.15
16. United Kingdom	5.04	44. U.S.S.R.	.13
17. Jordan	4.00	45. South Africa	.12
18. Finland	3.83	46. Colombia	.08
19. Syria	3.17	47. Peru	.07
20. Sweden	3.04	48. Brazil	.07
21. Singapore	3.00	49. Iran	.06
22. Australia	2.55	50. Thailand	.03
23. Kuwait	2.50	51. Indonesia	.03
24. Yugoslavia	2.34	52. Philippines	.00
25. United States	2.11	53. Pakistan	.01
26. Italy	1.90	54. India	.01
27. Bulgaria	1.86	55. Cyprus	.00
28. New Zealand	1.85		

Source: United Nations, 1976

Table 23: Country potential generation index

the correlation of higher educational attainment and the tendency to travel is very pronounced for travel south of the border.

The correlation of higher income levels and the greater tendency towards travel to the United States reflects a similar pattern to be found with education. For Canadians travelling to other countries, Ontario residents were by far the most likely to travel to other countries. Moreover, university graduates were by far the most likely candidates for travel to overseas destinations. For the non-travellers, the eastern region of Canada was the most likely place of residence for people who did not take a trip.

O'Leary et al. (1993) have also applied the idea of RPGI to develop a travel intensity index to study the travel flow of Canadian travellers by season and purpose of trip for both general and affluent travel markets. Table 25 presents the generated propensity to travel indices by region, season, and specific groups

Characteristics	Destination			
	Canada	United States	Other Countries	Non-travellers
Province of origin				
Newfoundland	81	16		155
Prince Edward Island	90	39	83	116
Nova Scotia	102	47		110
New Brunswick	96	61		189
Quèbec	94	80	87	114
Ontario	99	126	133	97
Manitoba	106	112		88
Saskachewan	122	73	82	69
Alberta	121	91		62
British Columbia	96	119	109	103
Age				
15–24	100	84	89	103
25–34	113	98	74	83
35–44	108	120	110	82
45–54	96	128	141	99
55–64	97	92	134	104
65+	75	83	123	148
Marital status				
Married	105	108	104	90
Single	97	94	97	107
Widowed	72	58	71	156
Separated/Divorced	91	80	93	119
Education				
1–8 years	73	59	72	155
Some secondary	98	91	79	103
Some postsecondary	115	105	91	77
Postsecondary certificate or diploma	122	151	128	54
University degree	122	167	242	52
Income				
Less than 9,000	72	38	37	161
9,000–14,999	82	59	43	136
15,000–19,999	98	80	75	109
20,000–24,999	105	88	55	99
25,000–29,999	107	95	79	86
30,000–34,999	119	137	117	57
35,000–39,999	124	136	111	54
More than 40,000	128	176	227	42
Occupation				
Professional	127	154	163	50
Clerical	113	135	133	67
Sales	107	113	73	81
Services	92	71	88	116
Primary	96	55	31	115
Manufacturing	92	77	82	114
Not in labor force	79	75	74	145

Source: McDougall, 1986

Table 24: Travel intensity index of Canada in 1984

ORIGIN	1ST QTR. Winter G	A	2ND QTR. Spring G	A	3RD QTR. Summer G	A	4TH QTR. Autumn G	A
East	1.13	0.78	0.88	0.31	1.03	0.67	0.95	0.67
Newfoundland	1.00	0.56	0.85	0.29	0.88	0.43	0.79	0.51
Prince Edward Island	0.80	0.33	0.54	0.13	0.53	0.19	0.35	0.17
Nova Scotia	1.26	1.00	1.05	0.37	1.25	0.96	1.07	0.84
New Brunswick	1.12	0.76	0.77	0.29	0.98	0.56	1.03	0.67
Middle	0.88	1.03	0.92	1.13	0.93	1.09	0.92	1.11
Quèbec	0.76	0.72	0.75	0.77	0.82	0.75	0.76	0.74
Ontario	0.97	1.24	1.04	1.39	1.01	0.56	1.02	1.38
West	1.22	1.00	1.22	0.91	1.14	0.89	1.20	0.84
Manitoba	1.07	0.52	1.19	0.47	1.36	0.97	1.27	0.65
Saskatchewan	1.96	1.39	1.57	1.19	1.38	0.73	1.68	0.67
Alberta	1.62	1.44	1.66	1.30	1.39	1.25	1.54	1.26
British Columbia	0.75	0.71	0.79	0.68	0.82	0.65	0.79	0.65

G represents *general;* A represents *affluent*
Index = 1.0 indicates an average generation capacity
Index > 1.0 indicates a region is generating more trips than its population
Index < 1.0 indicates a region is generating fewer trips than its population
Source: O'Leary et al., 1993

Table 25: Seasonal variation of propensity (RPGI) to travel in Canada

(general and affluent). For the general travel market, the West region showed the highest propensity in Canada.

Travellers from Saskatchewan and Alberta had higher travel propensities than other regions in different seasons. The index for Saskatchewan was almost 2, indicating the region had a very high generation capacity in the winter. This figure suggests that the area generated more trips than the population would suggest. Travellers from Prince Edward Island appeared to have less interest in traveling during the fall season.

In terms of affluent travellers, travel propensity varied in different regions and seasons. The middle region showed the highest propensity in Canada. Affluent travellers from Ontario, Alberta, and Saskatchewan had higher travel propensities than other regions. However, travellers from the East region showed less interest in travelling, especially travellers from Prince Edward Island, Newfoundland, and New Brunswick. This trend implies that if population is a measure of demand for travel, this region did not generate as much travel as it could have in 1990.

Relative to seasonal travel, the West region generated more affluent travel in the winter, while affluent travellers from the East region showed the least involvement in travelling in the spring season. Comparing general and affluent travellers, the West region showed the highest propensity for general travel in Canada, while the central region generated more trips than the population would suggest.

Uysal et al. (1995) followed O'Leary et al. (1993) and used the RPGI to study the travel flow of U.S.A. travellers by season and purpose of trip. Table 26 presents the generated propensity to travel by purpose of trip (pleasure and business). These indices are based on the number of projected trips provided in the Travel Survey Reports published by the USTDC.

The indices revealed interesting results. The Mountain West (Arizona, Colorado, Idaho, Montana, Nevada, New Mexico, Utah, and Wyoming) had the highest propensity to travel (1.72) for pleasure in winter, and for business in spring (1.72), suggesting that this region generates more trips than its population would suggest. The propensity to travel index of New England had the lowest (.55) travel generation power for business travel during the winter season.

It was also found that the region of East South Central (Alabama, Kentucky, Mississippi, and Tennessee) had the second highest travel generation index (1.30)

	Winter		Spring		Summer		Autumn	
ORIGIN	P	B	P	B	P	B	P	B
Northeast	0.90	0.67	0.86	0.90	0.90	0.95	0.86	0.86
New England	0.74	0.55	0.92	1.11	1.11	1.11	0.74	0.74
Mid-Atlantic	0.90	0.71	0.83	0.77	0.83	0.90	0.90	0.90
Southeast	1.01	0.93	1.09	1.05	0.97	0.84	0.88	0.97
South Atlantic	1.02	0.79	1.02	1.02	0.85	0.91	0.91	0.97
East South Central	0.98	1.30	1.30	0.98	1.30	0.65	0.81	0.98
Great Lakes	0.94	0.82	0.88	1.06	0.94	0.82	1.00	1.00
East North Central	0.94	0.82	0.88	1.06	0.94	0.82	1.00	1.00
Midwest	1.02	1.30	1.08	0.96	1.08	1.13	1.25	1.25
West South Central	0.96	1.43	1.05	0.76	1.15	1.05	1.43	1.15
West North Central	1.11	1.11	1.11	1.25	1.11	1.25	0.97	1.39
West	1.17	1.36	1.07	1.07	1.07	1.26	1.07	0.97
Mountain	1.72	1.53	1.34	1.72	1.53	1.91	1.34	1.34
Pacific	1.04	1.24	0.98	0.85	0.85	1.04	0.98	0.85

P represents *pleasure*; B represents *business*
Source: Uysal et al., 1995

Table 26: Seasonal variation in propensity to travel, 1989

for business travel in winter. In general, business travel appears to be very strong during the winter and summer seasons in the West region, and travel for pleasure shows a higher propensity in winter. West South Central (Arkansas, Louisiana, Oklahoma, and Texas) appeared to have had the highest travel generation index of 1.34 during the same season. It is important to note that the regional aggregation of states as travel regions may not reveal the true picture of state-specific spatial behaviors. Findings of the study, therefore, should be interpreted as showing trends rather than providing conclusive inferences about the spatial-use patterns of regions and states within the regions.

Destination Perception Index

The Destination Perception Index was developed by Rafferty (1990) to measure college students' perception of world regions as tourism destinations. The sum of the number of rankings multiplied by the rank was used to establish an index to rank the order of destination preference. According to this procedure, the region with the lowest index number was perceived to be the most attractive region for tourism; conversely, the region with the highest index number was considered to be the least attractive. The mathematical formula for the calculation is:

$$I = (xr)$$

where I is the Index number
x is the number of rankings for each rank
r is the rank number

The destination perception study developed by Rafferty's (1990) work was to assess the effects of instruction in geography on college students' perception of 12 world geographic regions as travel destinations before and after completing an introductory course in world regional geography. The results of the Destination Perception Index are presented in Table 27 and Table 28.

Directional Bias Index

The Directional Bias Index, developed by Wolfe (1966), is a simple measure of the vacation travel tendency for one particular direction. For example, the percentage of Canadians travelling south in winter is much higher than the number heading north. Vacation travel, whether that of individuals, groups, or entire population, often shows a predilection for one particular direction.

The Directional Bias Index is an origin-specific index because it summarizes the travel patterns of an origin with respect to each of its destinations (Smith, 1995). It can be used as one component of a large systematic description of the travel patterns of a region or population, or it can be used as an independent variable in modelling travel flows and in testing hypotheses about the forces affecting travel patterns. The formula of the Directional Bias Index is as follows:

$$D = \frac{10^5 (T_{ij})}{T_i \, T_j}$$

Region	Rank												Index	
	1	2	3	4	5	6	7	8	9	10	11	12	#	Rank
Pacific Isles	86	250	222	220	160	102	105	40	36	30	55	36	1342	1
Australia/N.Z.	100	204	207	212	175	144	105	64	90	50	22	12	1385	2
Western Europe	137	180	198	220	170	102	91	88	90	60	33	24	1393	3
Central America	9	84	33	256	340	306	329	280	198	140	88	12	2084	4
USA/Canada	38	76	123	220	275	270	266	168	162	150	176	444	2328	5
Eastern Europe	8	50	120	156	330	306	350	328	315	210	429	96	2693	6
N. Africa/M. East	2	14	27	12	65	90	182	352	468	890	847	984	1949	7
South America	4	12	22	112	160	324	490	568	522	340	253	216	3034	8
Eastern Asia	11	40	69	144	255	444	399	400	495	310	495	60	3122	9
Soviet Union	8	26	33	88	120	216	378	392	315	300	330	1464	3670	10
Southern Africa	7	14	24	24	70	102	245	352	468	610	1001	1140	4059	11
Southern Asia	0	2	9	16	15	156	126	312	612	1040	1188	672	4148	12

Source: Rafferty, 1990

Table 27: Destination perception index and rankings by region (beginning of semester)

Region	Rank												Index	
	1	2	3	4	5	6	7	8	9	10	11	12	#	Rank
Pacific Isles	86	250	222	220	160	102	105	40	36	30	55	36	1342	1
Australia/N.Z.	100	204	207	212	175	144	105	64	90	50	22	12	1385	2
Western Europe	137	180	198	220	170	102	91	88	90	60	33	24	1393	3
Central America	9	84	33	256	340	306	329	280	198	140	88	12	2084	4
USA/Canada	38	76	123	220	275	270	266	168	162	150	176	444	2328	5
Eastern Europe														
N. Africa/M. East	2	14	27	12	65	90	182	352	468	890	847	984	1949	7
South America	4	12	22	112	160	324	490	568	522	340	253	216	3034	8
Eastern Asia	11	40	69	144	255	444	399	400	495	310	495	60	3122	9
Soviet Union	8	26	33	88	120	216	378	392	315	300	330	1464	3670	10
Southern Africa	7	14	24	24	70	102	245	352	468	610	1001	1140	4059	11
Southern Asia	0	2	9	16	15	156	126	312	612	1040	1188	672	4148	12

Source: Rafferty, 1990

Table 28: Destination perception index and rankings by region (end of semester)

where D is the Directional Bias Index,
T_{ij} is the number of trips (person-trips, person-nights, or other appropriate unit) for trip from origin i to destination j,
T_i is the total number of trips from origin i to any destination,
T_j is the total number of trips from any origin to destination j,
10^5 is a scaling factor; any weight of appropriate size may be substituted as desired.

From Table 29 and Figure 10, the example (Smith, 1995) offer an illustration of the calculation of the Directional Bias Index. The data represent flows among four hypothetical origins and four destinations. Table 22 shows that the number of trip from origin A to destination B is 30. Origin A generates a total of 115 trips distributed over all destinations, while destination B receives 135 trips from all origins. By the above formula, the index values for trips from a to A is 300, a to B is 193, and so forth.

However, the index is only a measure of the proportion or relative distribution of trips from one region to each of its destinations (Smith, 1995). It does not reflect the net balance of travel between two regions. If the net flow is of interest, it must be calculated separately. It should be noted that net flow itself does not indicate a direction bias. Both statistics, net flow and direction bias, can be used together to obtain a fuller picture of travel flows than either would provide by itself.

Gross Travel Propensity (GTP)

Gross Travel Propensity is the other type of travel propensity developed by Schmidhauser (1975, 1976). It refers to the total number of trips taken in relation to the total population studied. It is analogous to the concept of "trip per capita," which also expresses trips as a ratio of the total population of the region in question (Van Doren and Stubbles, 1975).

$$GTP = \frac{TP}{P} * 100$$

where TP is the total number of trips undertaken by the population of the country or group.
P is the total population of the country or group.

Uysal, Oh, and O'Leary (1995) applied the idea of Gross Travel Propensity (GTP) and Region Potential Generation Index (RPGI) to study the travel flow of U.S. travellers. From Table 30, in 1989 the Mountain West (Arizona, Colorado, Idaho, Montana, Nevada, New Mexico, Utah, and Wyoming) had the highest propensity to travel year round in the U.S., suggesting that this region generates more trips than the population would suggest. The propensity to travel index of the Mid-Atlantic area (New Jersey, New York, and Pennsylvania) had the lowest travel generation power, suggesting that this region generates fewer trips than the population would suggest. Table 30 also reports the results of RPGI (Region Potential Generation Index) as defined earlier.

Origins *i*	*A*	*B*	*C*	*D*	ΣT*j* = *i*
a	50	30	10	25	115
b	60	90	15	5	170
c	10	10	80	15	115
d	25	5	30	75	135
ΣT*j*	*145*	*135*	*135*	*120*	

Source: Smith, 1995

Table 29: Data for calculation of a directional bias index

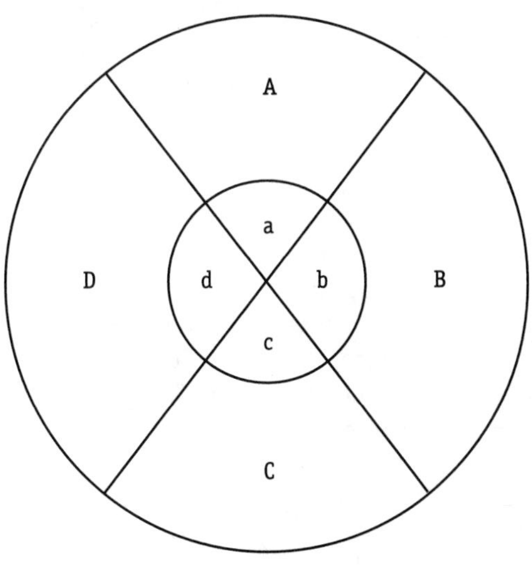

Source: Smith, 1995

Figure 10: A tourism system with four origins & four destinations

A closer examination of these indices also gives the same trends as the GTP figures. Pearson correlations were run between the two sets of indices to examine their association. Correlation coefficients were generated for each season. There was perfect correlation (*r* = 1.00) between the two propensity to travel measures. This indicates that these two indices measure the same underlying dimensions of propensity to travel and can be used interchangeably in the spatial study analysis of tourism.

	GTP				RPGI			
ORIGIN	Winter	Spring	Summer	Autumn	Winter	Spring	Summer	Autumn
Northeast	59.31	71.74	104.19	78.20	0.81	0.90	0.90	0.86
New England	54.15	87.91	127.68	67.43	0.74	1.11	1.10	0.74
Mid-Atlantic	61.15	66.17	96.11	81.99	0.83	0.83	0.83	0.90
Southeast	67.90	83.50	111.58	84.55	0.93	1.05	0.97	0.93
South Atlantic	66.59	81.08	104.68	82.92	0.91	1.02	0.91	0.91
E. S. Central	71.64	90.45	131.37	89.20	0.98	1.14	1.14	0.98
Great Lakes	68.92	74.58	101.56	91.18	0.94	0.94	0.88	1.00
E. N. Central	68.92	74.58	101.56	91.18	0.94	0.94	0.88	1.00
Midwest	83.01	80.85	130.48	108.53	1.13	1.02	1.13	1.19
W. S. Central	77.04	83.38	132.11	113.37	1.05	1.05	1.15	1.24
W. N. Central	81.51	77.18	128.12	101.49	1.11	0.97	1.11	1.11
West	89.16	84.91	117.72	97.70	1.22	1.07	1.02	1.07
Mountain	111.94	121.14	197.95	121.96	1.53	1.53	1.72	1.34
Pacific	81.37	72.52	105.33	89.40	1.11	0.91	0.91	0.98

New England: Connecticut, Maine, Massachusetts, New Hampshire, Rhode Island, Vermont.
Mid-Atlantic: New Jersey, New York, Pennsylvania
South Atlantic: Delaware, District of Columbia, Florida, Georgia, Maryland, North Carolina, South Carolina, Virgina, West Virgina
East South Central: Alabama, Kentucky, Mississippi, Tennessee
West South Central: Arkansas, Louisiana, Oklahoma, Texas
East North Central: Indiana, Illinois, Michigan, Ohio, Wisconsin
West North Central: Iowa, Kansas, Minnesota, Missouri, Nebraska, North Dakota, South Dakota
Mountain: Arizona, Colorado, Idaho, Montana, Nevada, New Mexico, Utah, Wyoming
Pacific: California, Oregon, Washington
Source: Uysal, Oh, and O'Leary, 1995

Table 30: Seasonal variation in propensity to travel, 1989

Main Destination Ratio (MDR)

The Main Destination Ratio is developed by Leiper (1989) to analyze "flows of travellers and tourists." Therefore, it can be defined as the percentage of arrivals by tourists in a given place for whom that place is the main or sole destination in the current trip, to the total arrival in that place. The MDR formula is presented as follows:

$$MDR = \frac{D_{ij}}{A_{ij}} * 100$$

where *MDR* is the Main Destination Ratio,
D_{ij} is the departures from the original place *i* to the main destination *j*,
A_{ij} is the total arrivals of *i* tourists in destination *j*.

Table 31 shows the MDR values and their derivations developed in Leiper's study (1989). The first column ("Departures . . . to Each Main Destination") comes from the data collected in the generating country where residents departing are required to nominate the country in which they will spend the longest time during their international trip. In certain countries, residents returning from trips abroad are asked to name which country they actually spent the most time visiting while away.

The second column ("Total Arrivals") comes from data collected in the destination country, where arriving visitors are required to state their country of residence. Figures in the third column ("Arrivals of Secondary . . . Tourists") are calculated by subtracting the first from the second column. These numbers represent tourists for whom that country is not the main but a secondary destination. The figures in the fourth column (MDR values) are calculated by comparing column one to column two, expressed as a percentage.

Another application of MDR in Leiper's study (1989) is in time series. Table 32 and Figure 11 provides illustrations, showing data about Australian residents' trips to Hong Kong and Singapore from 1975 to 1987. Trends in MDR values over 13 years leads to the conclusion that Hong Kong has made a significant gain in at least one area over Singapore.

Net Travel Propensity (NTP)

The Net Travel Propensity is a modification of TPI by Schmidhauser (1975, 1976). Net Travel Propensity refers to the proportion of the total population or a particular group in the population who have made at least one trip away from home in the period of question (usually a year).

$$NTP = \frac{p}{P} * 100$$

where p is the number of persons or in a particular population group who have made at least one trip away from home in a given period

P is the total population of the country or group

Recreation Index

Recreation Index is the modification of Defert's Tourist Function Index by Gardavsky (1977) to monitor whether the weekend recreation in Czechoslovakia involves occupying private chalets or cottages (second homes). Therefore, the Recreation Indices may be calculated by dividing the potential recreation area by the number of second homes. Gardavsky suggests that for a more meaningful appraisal of the distribution of second homes, it is not total area, but rather the potential recreation area available in each district which should be taken into account. This latter consists of "areas of woodland and water, in addition to orchards, parks, meadows, and pastures which contribute to the attractiveness of the environment for recreation." The term *recreation function* is used in an economic-geographical, not in an algebraic, sense in order to state mathematically something about the connection of a place's resident population in relation to the number of people who arrive for weekend recreation. The formula of the Recreation Index is:

Countries	Departures from Japan to Each Main Destination	Total Arrivals Japanese Tourists	Arrivals of 2nd Japanese Tourists	Main Destination Ratio
Taiwan	558	580	22	96
USA	1,389	1,447	58	96
Philippines	142	160	18	89
Korea	414	518	104	80
Australia	46	60	14	77
Hong Kong	329	515	186	64
UK	90	159	69	57
China	136	245	109	56
Singapore	189	378	189	50
Thailand	98	228	130	43
New Zealand	10	27	17	37
Canada	38	114	76	33
France	145	494	349	29
Germany (FR)	55	347	292	16
Switzerland	22	244	222	9
Italy	25	303	278	8
Sub-total	3,686	5,819	2,133	63
Other	400	NA	NA	NA
Total	4,086	NA	NA	NA

Source: Leiper, 1989

Table 31: Japanese visitors to selected countries in 1982

Countries	Main Destination Departures from AU to		Total Arrivals Of AU Visitors		Arrivals of AU Visitors		Main Destination Ratio	
	H.K.	Singapore	H.K.	Singapore	H.K.	Singapore	H.K.	Singapore
1975	30		127		97		24	
1976	40	43	157	216	117	173	25	20
1977	38	39	155	216	117	177	25	18
1978	40	39	164	229	124	190	24	17
1979	45	43	148	206	103	163	30	21
1980	58	59	171	239	113	180	34	25
1981	65	69	200	258	135	189	33	26
1982	73	71	197	281	124	210	37	25
1983	79	55	228	259	149	204	35	27
1984	96	61	278	291	182	230	35	21
1985	99	62	275	301	176	239	36	21
1986	119	81	276	316	157	235	43	26
1987	103	84	254	330	151	246	41	25

Source: Leiper, 1989

Table 32: Australian visitors in Hong and Singapore, 1975 to 1987 main destination ratio

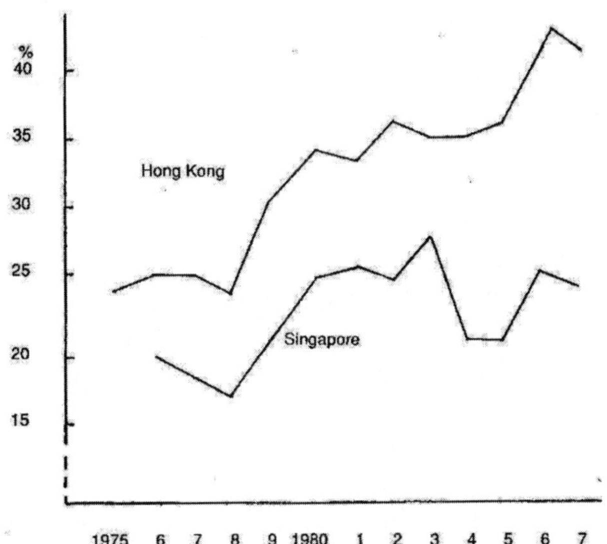

Source: Leiper, 1989

Figure 11: Main destination ratios of Australian visitors in Hong Kong and Singapore for the years 1975-1987

$$Rp_1 = \frac{L * 100}{O} * \frac{1}{Rp}$$

where Rp_1 is the Recreation Index,
L is the number of second homes multiplied by four, representing the average number of occupants,
O is the number of permanent residents,
Rp is the potential recreation area of the area surveyed.

An example of a Recreation Index developed by Gardavsky (1977) to monitor the weekend recreation in Czechoslovakia is presented in Figure 12. Before understanding of the recreation conditions in the districts of the Czech Socialist Republic can be developed, it is necessary to appreciate the range of values which might emerge.

1. Values 1–10 represent the initial stage of short-term recreational development. The term *initial stage* also suggests the possibility of further dynamic development taking place.
2. Values 11–30 represent the developing stage of short-term recreation. Even so, in some of these districts further development is not likely because of competition from industrial activity.
3. Values 31–90 represent the culminating stage. Further development of weekend recreation, and especially any further schemes for building second homes, will encounter serious problems and disadvantages.
4. Values 91–340 represent the overdeveloped stage of second-home establishment. These areas contain examples of land that has been degraded or even devastated for recreation purposes. Such areas are no longer suitable for weekend recreation, and it is necessary to make suitable arrangements for dealing with effluent if the quality of their environment is to be preserved.

Relative Acceptance Index (RAI)

The Relative Acceptance Index measures the relative success of a destination in attracting tourists from a generating country (Williams and Zelinsky, 1970). For instance, in the study of international tourist flow, RAI identifies major patterns in actual flows and is also useful to measure the magnitude of these against some predicted value in order to identify flows which might be stronger or weaker than expected.

The Relative Acceptance Index is computed by dividing the difference between actual and expected flows by the expected flow. This Relative Acceptance Index thus has a range from -1 to plus infinity. The lower value would occur if actual flows were zero. For the intermediate case, positive values indicate a greater than expected flow of tourists; negative values indicate the reverse. The results of the Relative Acceptance Index developed by Williams and Zelinsky (1970) represented the relative success or acceptance of a country as an attractive stopover point

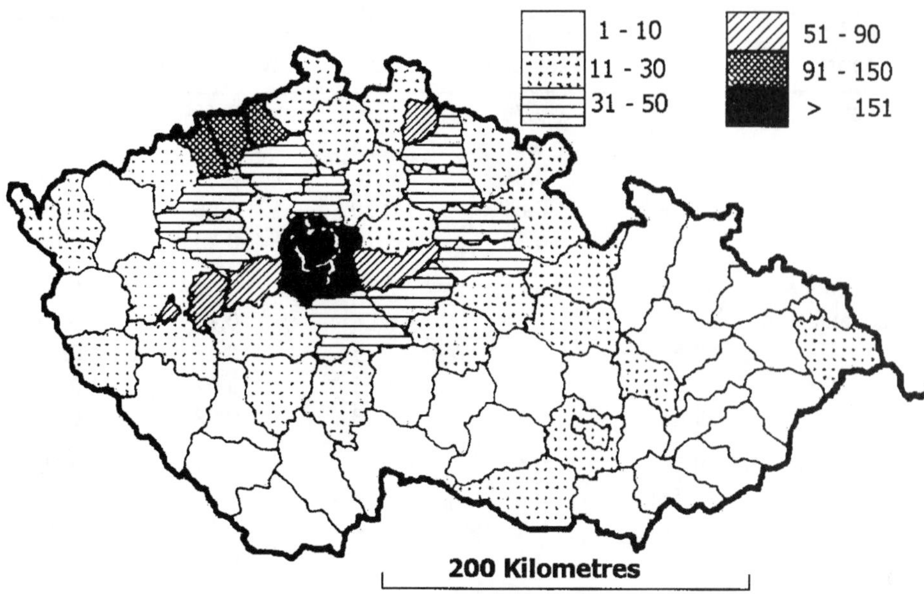

Source: Gardavsky, 1977

Figure 12: Recreation index in the Czech Socialist Republic

for tourists from the sending country. These are detailed in Table 33. The formula for the Relative Acceptance Index is:

$$RAI_{ij} = \frac{A_{ij} - E_{ij}}{E_{ij}} = \frac{\text{Actual flow from origin } i \text{ to destination } j}{\text{The expected flow from } i \text{ and } j}$$

where RAI_{ij} is the relative acceptance from origin i to destination j,
A_{ij} is the actual flow from origin i to destination j,
E_{ij} is the expected flow from i and j.

Moreover,

$$E_{ij} = \frac{n_i n_j}{n}$$

where n_i is the observed number of visitors from region i in the country as a whole,
n_j is the observed number of visitors in region j,
n is the total number of visitors in the country as a whole.

Sending Country	Receiving country: Austria	Belgium & Luxembourg	France	W. Germany	Greece
Austria	—	-0.76	-0.75	-0.42	-0.51
	—	-0.82	-0.73	0.34	-0.37
	—	-0.84	-0.70	-0.03	-0.12
	—	-0.81	-0.70	-0.08	-0.02
	—	-0.83	-0.71	-0.13	-0.01
Belgium & Luxembourg	-0.61	—	2.59	0.17	-0.47
	-0.64	—	2.14	0.10	-0.49
	-0.62	—	1.76	0.17	-0.45
	-0.59	—	1.75	0.07	-0.47
	-0.63	—	1.58	0.02	-0.51
France	-0.66	0.46	—	-0.51	0.09
	-0.58	0.80	—	-0.44	0.07
	-0.77	0.18	—	-0.54	-0.34
	-0.78	0.19	—	-0.58	-0.35
	-0.79	0.07	—	-0.61	-0.41
W. Germany	0.81	-0.59	-0.66	—	-0.47
	0.78	-0.65	-0.69	—	-0.51
	1.10	-0.59	-0.56	—	-0.44
	1.12	-0.56	-0.55	—	-0.48
	1.14	-0.51	-0.54	—	-0.50
Greece	0.04	-0.13	-0.20	0.30	—
	-0.07	0.02	-0.24	0.31	—
	-0.36	-0.28	—	0.31	—
	-0.32	-0.35	—	0.45	—
	-0.27	-0.33	—	0.44	—

Source: Williams and Zelinsky, 1970

Table 33: Relative deviations from expected flows for five selected years (1958–1966)

Tourism Location Score (TLS) and Familiarity Index

The Tourism Location Score was developed by Fridgen (1983, 1987) to compare tourism locations and counties in an attempt to provide a straightforward method of qualifying the data obtained from cognitive maps (see Figure 13). In contrast to hand-drawn sketch maps, several components of the task used in the study were easily observed and tallied: for example, the number of circles and Xs received by each county. Since the unit of analysis was individual counties, it was possible to tally the number of times a particular county was circled, received an X, and was partially circled (if a county was intersected by a circle, it was considered partially circled).

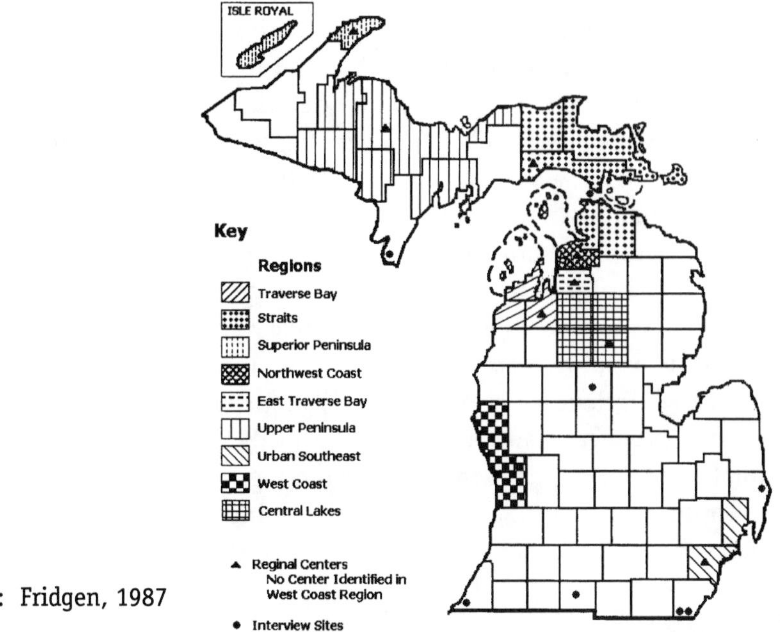

Source: Fridgen, 1987

Figure 13: Cognitive map of the state of Michigan

Then three map measures were integrated in the following way. First, the number of Xs given to all counties (A) by the total sample were counted. The number of times a county was completely circled was also divided by the total times all counties were circled yielding the map factor (B). The third measure, (C), the number of times a county was partially circled, was also divided by the total times all counties were partially circled across the sample. In essence, map factors A, B, and C represent ratios that can be compared across groups of respondents. With the ratio, it is possible to establish the relative importance of the three factors for a particular county relative to other counties considered by a particular sample or subsample.

Finally, weights were added to reflect the relative importance of a person's decision to place an X in the county, circle it entirely, or partially circle the county. Therefore, factors A and B were weighted the same, receiving a weight of 0.4, while factor C was weighted less, receiving a weight of 0.2. The higher the Tourism Location Score of the region, the more the respondents perceive it as a recreation and tourism region. The formula of the Tourism Location Score was as follows:

$$TLS = (.4A + .4B + .2C) * 1000$$

where *TLS* = Tourism Location Scores
A = the number of Xs given to all counties by the total sample
B = the number of times a county was completely circled divided by the total times all counties were circled
C = the number of times a county was partially circled divided by the total times all counties were partially circled across the sample

In the same study, Fridgen (1987) also developed a familiarity index by converting a five-point familiarity question (1—"not at all familiar" to 5—"extremely familiar") and the number of past trips in the state for recreation purposes into different three-point indices. For the familiarity question, the respondents who reported they were "not at all familiar" or "not very familiar" with the state of Michigan were given a score of 1; a score of 2 was assigned to those reporting that they were "somewhat familiar," while a 3 was assigned to those reporting that they were "very familiar" or "extremely familiar."

As for the number of past trips in the state for recreation purposes, first-time visitors were given a score of 1, those with two to five past visits received a score of 2, and those with six or more past visits received a score of 3. Combining the two sets of scores for each individual created a Familiarity Index ranging from 2 to 6. Those with a total between 2 and 4 were placed in the low familiarity category; those with total scores of 5 or 6 were place in the high familiarity category. The results of the Tourism Location Score by Familiarity Index are presented in Table 34. The formula of the Familiarity Index is:

$$FI = score(F) + score(T)$$

where *FI* = Familiarity Index;
if FI = 2/3/4, the respondents are placed in low familiarity category;
if FI = 5/6, the respondents are placed in high familiarity category.

County	Coastal (C) Inland (I)	Familiarity High	Familiarity Low	General Sample
Grand Traverse	C	75.0	44.6	67.7
Mackinac	C	58.4	90.7	65.6
Cheboygan	C	46.3	47.0	44.9
Leelanau	C	42.0	32.5	43.2
Keweenaw	C	39.0	33.9	32.4
Emmet	C	33.2	29.8	30.7
Chippewa	C	28.2	31.4	28.8
Charlevoix	C	27.2	19.3	24.7
Benzie	C	26.0	24.0	25.0
Antrim	C	21.9	9.2	16.5
Marquette	C	21.9	19.6	19.0
Clinton	I	1.6	4.6	3.4
Isabella	I	1.3	4.9	3.3
Branch	I	1.3	2.3	1.7
Gratiot	I	1.3	4.5	3.0
Ionia	I	0.5	1.0	0.9

Source: Fridgen, 1987

Table 34: Tourism location scores by familiarity

Moreover,

score(F) = 1, if A of familiarity Q is 1, "not at all familiar" or 2, "not very familiar";
= 2, if A of familiarity Q is 3, "somewhat familiar" ;
= 3, if A of familiarity Q is 4, "very familiar" or 5, "extremely familiar";

score(T) = 1, if # of past trips in the state for recreation purposes is 0;
= 2, if # of past trips in the state for recreation purposes is 2-5;
= 3, if # of past trips in the state for recreation purposes is 6/+.

Travel Propensity Index (TPI)

The Travel Propensity Index is an extension of the CPGI Index. Its assumption is that tourism is a function of population and person wealth, then by holding these two factors constant some measure of willingness or desire to travel can be established. This index was created by simply dividing the CPGI index by the per capita income of the respective country (Hudman, 1979). The higher the Travel Propensity Index is, the higher the degree of mobility (potential ability to travel). The results of Hudman's Travel Propensity Index study are presented in Table 35, and the formula is:

$$TPI = \frac{CPGI}{I}$$

where *CPGI* is the Country Potential Generation Index
I is the per capita income

1. Jordan	.0119	24. Egypt	.0006
2. Syria	.0101	25. Italy	.0006
3. Portugal	.0048	26. Australia	.0005
4. Ireland, Rep.	.0026	27. Greece	.0005
5. Germany, Fed. Rep.	.0023	28. New Zealand	.0005
6. Netherland	.0023	29. Saudi Arabia	.0005
7. Austria	.0020	30. Sweden	.0005
8. Luxembourg	.0018	31. Chile	.0003
9. Singapore	.0018	32. Kuwait	.0003
10. Turkey	.0018	33. Norway	.0003
11. Switzerland	.0017	34. United States	.0003
12. United Kingdom	.0017	35. Colombia	.0002
13. Belgium	.0016	36. Indonesia	.0002
14. Canada	.0016	37. Peru	.0002
15. Malaysia	.0016	38. Venezuela	.0002
16. Denmark	.0014	39. Brazil	.0001
17. France	.0012	40. Japan	.0001
18. Finland	.0011	41. Pakistan	.0001
19. Iraq	.0009	42. South Africa	.0001
20. Lebanon	.0009	43. Thailand	.0001
21. Mexico	.0009	44. Cyprus	.0000
22. Spain	.0008	45. India	.0000
23. Argentina	.0006	46. Iran	.0000

Source: United Nations, 1976

Table 35: Travel propensity index—Potential ability to travel

5

Price/Economic Indices

PRICE/ECONOMIC INDICES are the most significant for tourism economists and entrepreneurs to understand consumption and economic contributions of their tourism markets. In this Price/Economic Indices group, the Big Mac index is a lighthearted guide to whether currencies are at a "correct" level. It is not a precise predictor of currencies, but simply a tool to make exchange-rate theory a bit more digestible (*Economist*, 1995). The competitiveness index was developed to compare the price of Australian tourism services with the price of similar services in a range of competing destinations through the development of indices of international price competitiveness (Forsyth and Dwyer, 1996).

The Consumer Price Index (CPI) provides a commonly used measure of change in the aggregate price level of consumer goods and services; it yields timely information on price movements since it is available on a monthly basis and with a short time lag (Crawford, 1993). The Dow Jones Travel Index is developed to measure trends in air travel costs (*Wall Street Journal*, 1996). Relative price is used as an independent variable in models seeking to explain international travel from an origin (generating country) to a destination (receiving country) (Gray, 1966; Kwack, 1972; Diamond, 1977; Little, 1980; Loeb, 1982; Quayson and Var, 1982).

The spending index is to measure and monitor spending of overnight pleasure travel parties (Huan, 1997). The tourism impact factor is to measure the importance level of tourism to travelers by comparing travelers' travel expenditures to income; therefore, the tourism impact factor of a traveler is the ratio of per capita traveler expenditures to per capita personal income (Royer, McCool, and Hunt, 1974). The tourism proportion factor is developed to measure the importance level of tourism to regions (states) by comparing a region's overall travel expenditures to gross state product (income) (Royer, McCool, and Hunt, 1974). The index of tourist sales (total tourist spending) measures total tourist spending in Maine and the Canadian provinces (Sanders, Beard, Levesque, and Smith III, 1993).

The Travel Index uses expenditures (sales by hotels and motels) to measure tourism levels and reflects the importance of the hotel/motel tourism to the local economy (Judd and Rulison, 1983). The Travel Price Index was developed and published monthly by the U.S. Travel Data Center to measure the cost of the goods and services involved in the tourism industry because the industry includes a heterogeneous grouping of many industries (USTDC, 1989). All the original ideas, technical formula, statistical outputs, and applications of the indices in this Price/ Economic Indices group will be detailed in the following part of this section.

Big Mac Index (Big MacCurrencies)

The Big Mac index was devised in 1986 as a lighthearted guide to whether currencies are at a "correct" level. It is not a precise predictor of currencies, simply a tool to make exchange-rate theory a bit more digestible (*Economist*, 1995). *Burgernomics* is based upon one of the oldest concepts in international economic theory: the theory of purchasing-power parity (PPP). This holds that, in the long run, the exchange rate of two countries should move towards the rate that would equalize the prices of an identical basket of goods and services in each country. The "basket" of the Big Mac index is the McDonald's Big Mac: made to more or less the same recipe in 79 countries. The Big Mac PPP is the exchange rate that would leave hamburgers costing the same in America as abroad. Comparing actual exchange rates with PPP is one indication of whether a currency is under or over value. However, as mention above, the Big Mac PPPs are only a handy guide to the cost of living in countries, they may not be a reliable guide to exchange rate (*Economist*, 1995). The 1995 Big Mac index is presented in Table 36 and its formula is as follows:

$$\text{BMI} = \text{Local currency under-/over-valuation, \%}$$

$$= \frac{\text{Implied PPP of the dollars}}{\text{Actual \$ exchange rate}} \quad \text{(PPP is Purchasing-Power Parity)}$$

moreover,

$$\text{Implied PPP of the dollars} = \frac{\text{Big Mac price in local currency}}{\text{Big Mac price in the United States}}$$

From the first column of Table 36, the cheapest Big Mac is in China: it costs \$1.05, compared with an average price in four American cities of \$2.32 (all prices include sales tax). At the other extreme, Big Mac munchers in Switzerland pay a beefy \$5.20. This is another way of saying that yuan is the most undervalued currency, the Swiss franc the most overvalued. The third column calculates Big Mac PPPs. For example, dividing the Japanese price by the American one gives a dollar PPP of ¥169. On April 7, the rate was ¥84, implying that the yen is 100% overvalued against the dollar—or looking at it from the other point of view, that the dollar is 50% undervalued (*Economist*, 1995).

The Hamburger Standard					
	Big Mac Prices		Implied	Actual $	Local Currency
	In Local Currency	In Dollars	PPP of the Dollar	Exchange Rate 7/4/95	under(-)/over(+) Valuation, %
UNITED STATES	$2.32	$2.32	—	—	—
Argentina	Peso3.00	3.00	1.29	1.00	+29
Australia	A$2.45	1.82	1.06	1.35	-22
Austria	Sch39.0	4.01	16.80	9.72	+73
Belgium	Bfr109	3.84	47.00	28.40	+66
Brazil	Real2.42	2.69	1.04	0.90	+16
Britain	£1.74	2.80	1.33	1.61	+21
Canada	C$2.77	1.99	1.19	1.39	-14
Chile	Peso950	2.40	409.00	395.00	+4
China	Yuan9.00	1.05	3.88	8.54	-55
Czech Republic	Ckr50.0	1.91	21.60	26.20	-18
Denmark	Dkr26.75	4.92	11.50	5.43	+112
France	Ffr18.5	3.85	7.97	4.80	+66
Germany	DM4.80	3.48	2.07	1.38	+50
Holland	FI5.45	3.53	2.35	1.55	+52
Hong Kong	HK$9.50	1.23	4.09	7.73	-47
Hungary	Forint191	1.58	82.30	121.00	-32
Indonesia	Rupiah3,900	1.75	1681.00	2231.00	-25
Israel	Shekel8.90	3.01	3.84	2.95	+30
Italy	Lire4,500	2.64	1940.00	1702.00	+14
Japan	¥391	4.65	169.00	84.20	+100
Malaysia	M$3.76	1.51	1.62	2.49	-35
Mexico	Peso10.9	1.71	4.70	6.37	-26
New Zealand	NZ$2.95	1.96	1.27	1.51	-16
Poland	Zloty3.40	1.45	1.47	2.34	-37
Russia	Rouble8,100	1.62	3491.00	4985.00	-30
Singapore	S$2.95	2.10	1.27	1.40	-9
South Korea	Won2,300	2.99	991.00	769.00	+29
Spain	Ptas355	2.86	153.00	124.00	+23
Sweden	Skr26.0	3.54	11.20	7.34	+53
Switzerland	Sfr5.90	5.20	2.54	1.13	+124
Taiwan	NT$65.0	2.53	28.00	25.70	+9
Thailand	Baht48.0	1.95	20.70	24.60	-16

Source: McDonald's; *Economist*, 1995

Table 36: The Big Mac index, 1995

Competitiveness Index

The competitiveness index was developed by Forsyth and Dwyer (1996) to compare the price of Australian tourism services with the price of similar services in a range of competing destinations through the development of indices of international price competitiveness. In short, the tourism competitiveness index is used to obtain a measure of the real price of buying tourism goods and services in different countries at a given point in time. Forsyth and Dwyer (1996) developed the prices of goods and services typically purchased by tourists, and found out their prices in each country. The travel/tourism prices of goods and services for each country were obtained from the 255 separate price categories published by the World Bank.

In short, the travel/tourism prices were calculated by weighting (multiplying) the expenditure shares typical of a tourist from a given country by the prices of the different goods and services as reported by the World Bank. Therefore, the competitiveness index is the comparison between the prices faced in Australia by a tourist from a particular country and the local prices. The bilateral price comparisons between Australia and other countries are presented in Table 37. The formula is as follows:

$$CI = \frac{TPI(J)}{TPI(A)}$$

where *CI* = competitiveness index
TPI(J) = travel price of country *J*
TPI(A) = Travel price of Australia

and,

TPI = (255 separate price categories)*
(expenditure share of a tourist from a given country)

In Table 37, the competitiveness index value of Germany in 1995 is more than 1 (1.596); it means that the goods and services bought by a visitor will cost more in Germany than in Australia. In this example Australia has become a more attractive destination for the German tourists; Australian prices are very low for German tourists.

Consumer Price Indices (CPI)

The present Consumer Price Index (CPI) formerly called the "Cost of Living," was initiated at the time of World War I for use in wage negotiation (United States Department of Labor, 1966). The Consumer Price Index (CPI) provides a commonly used measure of change in the aggregate price level of consumer goods and services. It yields timely information on price movements since it is available on a monthly basis and with a short time lag (Crawford, 1993).

Today, the Consumer Price Index fills the different needs of its many different users. The country's principal measure of price change, the index is used (1) as an

	1985	1990	1993	1995
Australia	1.000	1.000	1.000	1.000
New Zealand	0.740	0.867	0.935	1.044
United States	1.280	1.004	1.136	1.029
Canada	1.209	1.100	1.149	0.971
Germany	1.125	1.359	1.587	1.596
Spain	0.816	0.946	1.159	1.016
United Kingdom	1.049	1.156	1.206	1.207
Japan	1.300	1.379	2.096	2.052
Korea	0.581	0.653	0.704	0.686
Sri Lanka	0.568	0.456	0.529	0.490
India	0.621	0.603	0.483	0.485
Hong Kong	1.044	0.960	1.372	1.397
Malaysia	0.607	0.427	0.520	0.564
Singapore	0.890	0.745	0.942	1.042
Indonesia	0.435	0.255	0.314	0.334
China	0.224	0.130	0.159	0.149
Thailand	0.670	0.592	0.684	0.649

Source: Forsyth and Dwyer, 1996

Table 37: Competitiveness index between Australia and other countries

indicator of inflation to evaluate economic policy—during periods of price rise, it is an index of inflation and serves as an economic indicator to measure the success or failure of government economic policy; (2) as a deflator to adjust other economic indicators, such as Gross National Product, and to adjust other series for price changes and to translate these series into inflation-free dollars; and (3) as a monitor of how well income payments keep up with the cost of living—to escalate income payments. (United States Department of Labor, 1978).

The formula of the Consumer Price Index developed by the United States Department of Labor (1966) is as follows:

$$I_i = \frac{(P_o Q_a)(P_i/P_o)}{(P_o Q_a)} * 100$$

where *i* is the current month

a is the period of the most recent expenditure survey (1960–61) from which current weights were derived

o is the reference base period of the index (most recently 1957–59)

q is a derived composite of the annual quantities purchased in a weight base period for a bundle of goods and services to be represented by the specific item priced

p is the average price of a specific commodity or service selected for pricing

In 1978, with the continually growing uses and users of the Consumer Price Index, the Bureau of Labor Statistics (United States Department of Labor, 1978) introduced a new Consumer Price Index for All Urban Consumers (CPI-U). This covered 80 percent of the total population and a revised CPI for urban wage earners and clerical worker families and single persons (revised CPI-W) covering about half the CPI-U population. Both formulas of the old CPI and the new CPI (CPI-U; CPI-W) are exactly the same but only the study populations are different. The base year of both old and new CPI is 1967 (= 100). The table of some adjusted consumer price indices is shown in Appendix A.

In the travel and tourism industry, the Consumer Price Index is as important as the Travel/Tourism Price Index and can be used to estimate the Travel/Tourism Price Index. Morley (1994) investigated evidence for the use of CPI for tourism prices, employing a variety of methods and data. For 10 important tourist destinations, price series for major tourist expenditure items (hotel accommodation, restaurant meals and travel) were estimated. These tourism prices were found, with a few exceptions, to correlate very highly with the destination's CPI; the high correlations persisted even after linear time-trend effects were removed from the series (Table 38).

Moreover, in Morley's same study, detailed Australia data on tourist origins, numbers, spending breakdowns, and price changes were used to derive sound tourism price indices for major origins of tourists to Australia. The results (see Table 39) also show that the Australian Tourism Price Indices and Consumer Price Index are highly correlated and confirm that it is reasonable to use CPI as a proxy for tourism prices in a demand model.

Dow Jones Travel Index

Dow Jones Travel Index is developed to measure trends in air travel costs (*Wall Street Journal*, 1996). For example, the business air fare changed from $930 in the first week of November 1995 to $820 in the first week of November 1996. Therefore, the Dow Jones Travel Index in business air fare is 13% [(930 - 820) * 100/820 = 13%]. Moreover, the leisure air fare changed from $420 in the first week of November, 1995 to $430 in the first week of November, 1996. The Dow Jones Travel Index in leisure air fare is 2% [(430 - 420) * 100/420 = 2%].

The trends in travel costs expressed by the Dow Jones Travel Index are presented in Figure 14 and the formula is following.

$$DJTI_i = \frac{S_i - P_i - 1}{P_i - 1} * 100$$

where $DJTI_i$ is the Dow Jones Travel Index in the *i*th week of the study year
S_i is the business/leisure fare in the *i*th week of the study year
P_i is the business/leisure fare in the *i*th week of the previous year

Price Index Series	Time-Trend Effects ->	Correlation with CPI (1) Not Removed	Correlation with CPI (2) Removed
Canada Hotel		0.990	0.400
Canada Restaurant		0.999	0.783
Canada Travel		0.999	0.930
France Hotel		0.996	0.882
France Restaurant		0.991	0.946
Germany Hotel		0.988	0.201
Germany Restaurant		0.992	0.838
Germany Travel		0.993	0.888
Italy Hotel		0.999	0.984
Italy Restaurant		0.999	0.990
Italy Travel		0.999	0.932
Spain Hotel		0.992	0.274
Spain Travel		1.000	0.917
Sweden Hotel		0.996	0.953
Sweden Restaurant		0.993	0.848
Swiss Hotel		0.972	0.031
Swiss Restaurant		0.995	0.719
Turkey Hotel		0.995	0.992
UK Hotel		0.984	0.414
UK Restaurant		0.995	0.841
UK Travel		0.998	0.899
Yugoslavia Hotel		1.000	1.000

Source: Morley, 1994

Table 38: Tourism/travel price indices and CPI

Origin	Time-Trend Effects ->	Correlation with CPI (1) Not Removed	Correlation with CPI (2) Removed
USA		0.998	0.834
Japan		0.996	0.637
New Zealand		0.996	0.687
United Kingdom		0.998	0.806
Germany		0.998	0.851
Canada		0.997	0.718

Source: Morley, 1994

Table 39: Correlation of Australian tourism prices and CPI

Relative Price Index (RPI)

Relative price has frequently been used as an independent variable in models seeking to explain international travel from an origin (generating country) to a destination (receiving country) (Gray, 1966; Kwack, 1972; Diamond, 1977; Little, 1980; Loeb, 1982; Quayson and Var, 1982).

These models indicate that tourists are likely to respond when there is a change in the ratio between prices in a tourism-exporting country relative to prices in an importing country or prices in alternative tourist destinations. Thus, if relative prices "decline" between a generating and a destination country, an "increase" in the quantity of international tourism services purchased by the tourism-generating country should be anticipated, other things being equal (Uysal and Crompton, 1985).

Relative price is usually input into a forecasting model in the form of an index which reflects prices in the generating countries relative to those in the destination country. Studies reported in the travel/tourism literature which have used relative price index as an independent variable typically have not employed it as a simple ratio between an origin and a destination; rather, it has been weighted (Uysal and Crompton, 1985). Because overseas tourists frequently include more than one country in their itineraries, a higher-than-expected price level in one country may result in less time being spent in that country and compensatory time and money being spent in another country (Gray, 1966).

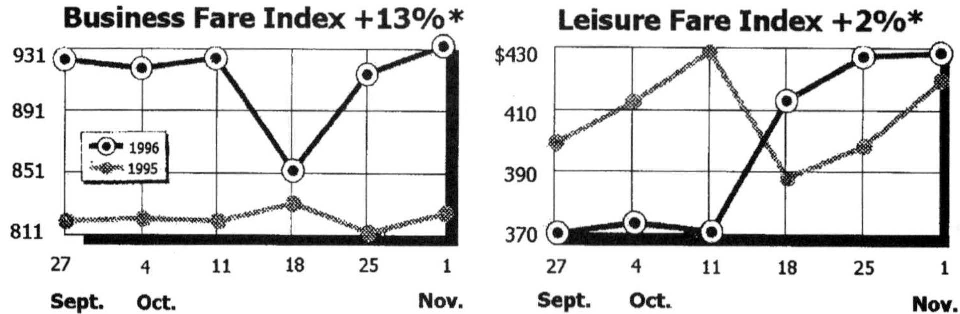

*Percent change from the first week of November 1995 to the first week of November 1996

Source: *Wall Street Journal,* 1996

Figure 14: Dow Jones Travel Index—trends in air travel costs

As mentioned above, the relative price index is used to estimate tourism demand by its weighting indices. There are two basic approaches to measuring the relative price index: (1) market share weighting (Joseph and Judd, 1974; Witt and Martin, 1987), to weight prices by market share and allow for changes in the attractiveness of destinations to consumers to be included; and (2) judgmental evaluation of competitive power (Uysal and Crompton, 1987; Uysal and Crompton, 1985), to weight the attractiveness of destinations by a judgmental evaluation of the competitive powers of the destination. This coincides with the rank of their respective distances from a destination.

As for competitive power weighting, in the relative price study by Uysal and Crompton (1985), the origin country's weight was given a value of 0.5, because home tourism is an important source of competition for foreign tourism. The remaining 0.5 value was divided among the generating countries. It was allocated according to their competitive rank. In terms of their relative competitiveness as alternative destinations to Turkey, the 11 countries were ranked as follows: Greece, Yugoslavia, Italy, France, Spain, West Germany, Austria, Switzerland, United Kingdom, United States, and Canada. This order almost coincides with the rank of their respective distance from Turkey. The derivation of the "weights" for each of the tourist-generating countries was as follows:

Austria	= CPIA * 0.5 + CPIG * 0.09 + CPIY * 0.08 + CPII * 0.07 + CPIF * 0.06 + CPIS * 0.06 + CPIWG * 0.04 + CPISW * 0.04 + CPIUK * 0.03 + CPIUSA * 0.02 + CPIC * 0.01
Canada	= CPIC * 0.5 + CPIG * 0.09 + CPIY * 0.08 + CPII * 0.07 + CPIF * 0.06 + CPIS * 0.06 + CPIWG * 0.04 + CPIA * 0.04 + CPISW * 0.03 + CPIUK * 0.02 + CPIUSA*0.01
France	= CPIF * 0.5 + CPIG * 0.09 + CPIY * 0.08 + CPII * 0.07 + CPIS * 0.06 + CPIWG * 0.06 + CPIA * 0.04 + CPISW * 0.04 + CPIUK * 0.03 + CPIUSA * 0.02 + CPIC * 0.01
Greece	= CPIG * 0.5 + CPIY * 0.09 + CPII * 0.08 +CPIF * 0.07 + CPIS * 0.06 + CPIWG * 0.06 + CPIA * 0.04 + CPISW * 0.04 + CPIUK * 0.03 + CPIUSA * 0.02 + CPIC * 0.01
Italy	= CPII * 0.5 + CPIG * 0.09 + CPIY * 0.08 + CPIF * 0.07 + CPIS * 0.06 + CPIWG * 0.06 + CPIA * 0.04 + CPISW * 0.04 + CPIUK * 0.03 + CPIUSA * 0.02 + CPIC * 0.01
Spain	= CPIS * 0.5 + CPIG * 0.09 + CPIY * 0.08 + CPII * 0.07 + CPIF * 0.06 + CPIWG * 0.06 + CPIA * 0.04 + CPISW * 0.04 + CPIUK * 0.03 + CPIUSA * 0.02 + CPIC * 0.01
Switzer-land	= CPISW * 0.5 + CPIG * 0.09 + CPIY * 0.08 + CPII * 0.07 + CPIF * 0.06 + CPIS * 0.06 + CPIWG * 0.04 + CPIA * 0.04 + CPIUK * 0.03 + CPIUSA * 0.02 + CPIC * 0.01
West Germany	= CPIWG * 0.5 + CPIG * 0.09 + CPIY * 0.08 + CPII * 0.07 + CPIF * 0.06 + CPIS * 0.06 + CPISW * 0.04 + CPIA * 0.04 + CPIUK * 0.03 + CPIUSA * 0.02 + CPIC * 0.01
United Kingdom	= CPIUK * 0.5 + CPIG * 0.09 + CPIY * 0.08 + CPII * 0.07 + CPIF * 0.06 + CPIS * 0.06 + CPIWG * 0.04 + CPIA * 0.04 + CPISW * 0.03 + CPIUSA * 0.02 + CPIC * 0.01
United States	= CPIUSA * 0.5 + CPIG * 0.09 + CPIY * 0.08 + CPII * 0.07 + CPIF * 0.06 + CPIS * 0.06 + CPIWG * 0.04 + CPIA * 0.04 + CPISW * 0.03 + CPIUK * 0.02 + CPIC * 0.01
Yugo-slavia	= CPIY * 0.5 + CPIG * 0.09 + CPII * 0.08 + CPIF * 0.07 + CPIS * 0.06 + CPIWG * 0.06 + CPISW * 0.04 + CPIA * 0.04 + CPIUK * 0.03 + CPIUSA * 0.02 + CPIC * 0.01

where *CPIA* = Consumer price index of Austria
CPIC = Consumer price index of Canada
CPIF = Consumer price index of France
CPIG = Consumer price index of Greece
CPII = Consumer price index of Italy
CPIS = Consumer price index of Spain
CPISW = Consumer price index of Switzerland
CPIWG = Consumer price index of West Germany
CPIUK = Consumer price index of the United Kingdom
CPIUSA = Consumer price index of the United States
CPIY = Consumer price index of Yugoslavia

After the weights had been obtained for each of the tourist-generating countries versus Turkey, the following index was derived:

$$RPI = \frac{CPI_R \,/\, EXR_R}{\sum_{i=1}^{n} WCPIA_G}$$

where *RPI* is relative price index,
CPIR is Consumer Price Index of the receiving country,
EXRR is exchange rate of the receiving country,
WCPIAG is the weighted consumer price indicing countries.

As for market-share weighting, Witt and Martin (1987) followed the work of Uysal and Crompton (1985), derived a different weighting technique, and stated that a change in tourist prices in Canada now has no effect on tourist flows from the United Kingdom to Turkey, whereas it has a substantial impact on tourist flows from the United States to Turkey. Therefore, Witt and Martin (1987) proclaimed that the weights in any given year may be calculated from the average market shares of destination countries over the previous years (See Tables 40 and 41).

Spending Index

The spending index was developed by Huan (1997) to measure and monitor the spending of U.S. Great Lakes region, overnight pleasure-travel parties in Ontario, Canada. In the study, the data were collected by Statistics Canada through the International Travel Survey looking at travel parties from other countries. The spending indices for (1) Accommodations, (2) Transportation, (3) Food/Beverage, (4) Recreation/Entertainment, and (5) Other are:

$$\text{spending index: } \frac{\text{Spending for specific items}}{\text{Total spending}} * 100$$

* The consuming index could be for (1) Accommodations, (2) Transportation, (3) Food/Beverage, (4) Recreation/Entertainment, and (5) Other.

These spending indices showed the importance levels of different types of spending in the area for U.S. overnight pleasure travellers. In Table 42 and Figure 15, "Accommodation" was the most important expenditure category for U.S. travellers, especially in winter (from January to March). This finding is reasonable because the index for "hotel" increased in fall and winter but decreased in spring and summer; conversely, the indices of "Cottage or Cabin" and "Camping" increased in spring and summer but decreased in fall and winter.

"Food and Beverage" was the second most important spending category. In some seasons (summer and fall 1992), "Food and Beverage" was even more important than "Accommodation."

Destination	Visits (000)	Weights
Austria	433	0.04
Belgium/Luxembourg	487	0.04
France	3,883	0.32
German Federal/Republic	397	0.03
Gibraltar/Malta/Cyprus	377	0.03
Greece	816	0.07
Italy	843	0.07
Netherlands	362	0.03
Portugal	504	0.04
Spain	3,986	0.33

Source: Witt and Martin, 1987

Table 40: Tourist visits abroad by United Kingdom residents in 1983

Destination	Visits (000)	Weights
Austria	551	0.02
Canada	10,913	0.49
France	1,270	0.06
German Federal/Republic	1,118	0.05
Italy	877	0.04
Mexico	3,900	0.17
Netherlands	521	0.02
Spain	385	0.02
Switzerland	791	0.04
United Kingdom	1,918	0.09

Source: Witt and Martin, 1987

Table 41: Tourist visits abroad by United States residents in 1983

Table 42: Spending index of U.S. Great Lakes region travellers in Ontario

	Spending Index of Spamt					
	1	2	3	4	5	
1990 Jan-Mar	31.91	8.39	26.90	11.08	10.75	
1990 Jan-Mar	31.51	8.78	25.95	11.90	9.47	
1990 Jul-Sep	30.75	8.30	27.04	12.22	11.20	
1990 Oct-Dec	27.77	5.54	26.39	10.96	11.59	Spending
1991 Jan-Mar	36.54	5.24	27.26	11.51	10.26	
1991 Apr-Jun	29.09	9.17	26.72	13.75	9.00	1. Accommodation
1991 Jul-Sep	30.90	8.11	23.56	13.46	8.27	
1991 Oct-Dec	27.29	6.21	25.94	16.54	13.00	2. Transportation
1992 Jan-Mar	34.60	5.10	29.57	17.65	8.14	
1992 Apr-Jun	28.43	6.30	24.67	13.10	11.71	3. Food/Beverage
1992 Jul-Sep	29.05	8.28	30.16	13.97	10.45	
1992 Oct-Dec	26.56	5.46	27.42	15.14	11.49	4. Recreation/
1993 Jan-Mar	28.30	8.33	23.86	15.19	8.38	Entertainment
1993 Apr-Jun	27.52	6.84	23.53	14.06	10.60	
1993 Jul-Sep	30.07	8.32	25.26	14.13	9.63	5. Other
1993 Oct-Dec	21.44	5.12	20.88	15.77	12.16	(souvenirs,
1994 Jan-Mar	31.61	6.80	25.52	14.43	8.80	shopping,
1994 Apr-Jun	32.23	7.50	22.63	13.09	9.13	photo, etc.)
1994 Jul-Sep	31.58	7.36	26.06	11.50	10.71	
1994 Oct-Dec	28.94	6.68	23.01	11.68	13.98	
1995 Jan-Mar	31.44	7.08	25.30	15.71	7.76	
1995 Apr-Jun	27.59	9.47	23.22	13.91	9.71	
1995 Jul-Sep	29.31	8.03	24.08	12.02	11.24	
1995 Oct-Dec	29.00	7.15	22.85	11.97	13.55	

Source: Huan, 1997

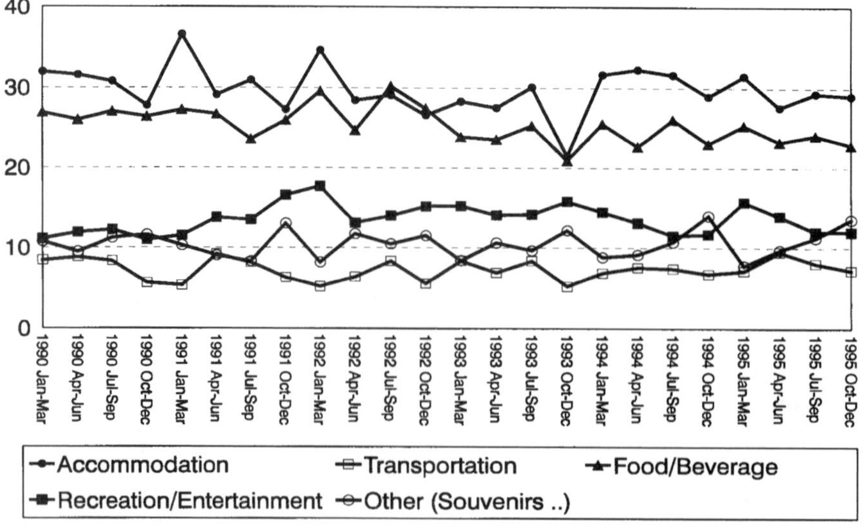

Source: Huan, 1997

Figure 15: Spending index of U.S. Great Lakes region travellers in Ontario

"Recreation and Entertainment" was the third most important category and its seasonal change was not significant.

Tourism Impact Factor (TIF)

The tourism impact factor was developed by Royer, McCool, and Hunt (1974) to measure the importance level of tourism to travellers by comparing travellers' travel expenditure to income. Therefore, the tourism impact factor of a traveller is the ratio of per capita traveller expenditures to per capita personal income. This suggests the relative weight of tourism expenditures to individual wealth. The higher the tourism impact factor score is, the more important tourism is to the traveller. Some of the tourism impact factors are presented in Table 43, and its formula is:

$$TIF = \frac{E}{I} * 100$$

where *E* is per capita tourism expenditures,
I is per capita personal income.

Tourism Proportion Factor (TPF)

The tourism proportion factor is developed by Royer, McCool, and Hunt (1974) to measure the importance level of tourism to regions (states) by comparing a region's overall travel expenditures to gross state product (income). Therefore, the ratio of gross traveller expenditures to gross state product is an indicator of the relative importance of tourism to the state's economy (Royer, McCool, and Hunt, 1974). The higher tourism proportion factor score it is, the more importance of the tourism industry to the region (state). Some of the tourism proportion factors are presented in Table 44, and its formula is as follows:

$$TPF = \frac{E}{P} * 100$$

where *E* is per capita tourism expenditures,
P is gross state product.

Tourist Sales (TS)

The index of tourist sales (total tourist spending) was developed by Sanders, Beard, Levesque, and Smith III (1993) to measure total tourist spending in Maine and the Canadian provinces. The tourist sales generated by visitors were regarded as the excess of monthly sales in the other 11 months over the base of native sales; and, the lowest tourist month in the year, January, is chosen as the base year, as it represents sales generated "almost entirely by local residents."

$$TS = S\sum_{n=1}^{12} (S_i - S_{Jan.})$$

	Gross State Product $billions	Per Capita Personal Income $thousands	Traveller Expenditure $millions	Population In 1970 $thousands	Per Capita Traveller Expenditure	Tourism Impact Factor
Alabama	11.6	2.828	313.9	3,444.1	91.14	3.22
Alaska	1.7	4.676	189.2	302.1	626.28	13.39
Arizona	6.1	3.542	619.1	1,772.4	349.30	9.68
Arkansas	6.1	2.742	328.8	1,923.2	170.96	6.20
California	84.0	4.469	4,094.8	19,953.1	205.22	4.52
Colorado	10.1	3.751	781.8	2,207.2	354.20	9.39
Connecticut	12.3	4.807	285.1	3,032.2	94.02	1.95
Delaware	2.7	4.233	112.8	548.1	205.80	4.83
Florida	26.4	3.584	3,382.7	6,789.4	498.23	4.23
Georgia	16.6	3.277	714.9	4,589.5	155.76	4.73
W. Virginia	5.5	2.929	239.9	1,744.2	137.54	18.76
Wisconsin	17.3	3.722	907.0	4,417.9	205.30	5.52
Wyoming	1.6	3.420	152.1	332.4	457.58	13.38

Source: Royer, McCool, and Hunt, 1974

Table 43: Relative importance of tourism to travellers by state

where TS is the yearly tourist sales,
S_i is the sales tax receipts in month i,
$S_{Jan.}$ is sales taxes in January.

The tourism spending in the study of Sanders et al. (1993) was based on "profits" but not on gross spending data. The profits were measured as the sum of sales taxes, state income taxes, and profits to the private operator, net of any taxes and operating expenses. At the core of a total tourist spending model to measure tourism spending profits is the system of accounts maintained by the sales tax department of the state of Maine. The broad categories of these accounts selected in this study are lodging, restaurants, other retail, food stores, general merchandise, and gas tax. However, building supplies, auto transportation, and business operating are excluded. Utilizing the formula of yearly tourist sales and the various sales tax categories, annual sales are given in Table 45, column 7.

Travel Index (TI)

The Travel Index is similar to the Travel Function. The Travel Index uses expenditures (sales by hotels and motels) to measure tourism levels. In the same way as the Travel Function, the Travel Index also can reflect the importance of the hotel/motel tourism to the local economy (Judd and Rulison, 1983). The formula of the Travel Index is:

$$TI_{SA} = \frac{TI_C}{SF} * 100$$

	Gross State Product $billions	Per Capita Personal Income $thousands	Traveller Expenditure $millions	Population In 1970 $thousand	Per Capita Traveller Expenditure	Tourism Proportion Factor
Alabama	11.6	2.828	313.9	3,444.1	91.14	2.71
Alaska	1.7	4.676	189.2	302.1	626.28	11.13
Arizona	6.1	3.542	619.1	1,772.4	349.30	10.15
Arkansas	6.1	2.742	328.8	1,923.2	170.96	7.50
California	84.0	4.469	4,094.8	19,953.1	205.22	4.70
Colorado	10.1	3.751	781.8	2,207.2	354.20	7.70
Connecticut	12.3	4.807	285.1	3,032.2	94.02	2.31
Delaware	2.7	4.233	112.8	548.1	205.80	4.16
Florida	26.4	3.584	3,382.7	6,789.4	498.23	3.87
Georgia	16.6	3.277	714.9	4,589.5	155.76	4.30
W. Virginia	5.5	2.929	239.9	1,744.2	137.54	4.35
Wisconsin	17.3	3.722	907.0	4,417.9	205.30	5.23
Wyoming	1.6	3.420	152.1	332.4	457.58	9.50

Source: Royer, McCool, and Hunt, 1974

Table 44: Relative importance of tourism to state

where TI_{SA} is seasonally adjusted Travel Index,
SF is seasonal factor carried out using the X-11 seasonal adjustment program developed by the U.S. Department of Commerce and available for use with the SAS system (SAS Institute, 1980),
TI_C is crude Travel Index, and

$$TI_C = \frac{SA}{IB} * 100$$

where IB is the index base,
SA is adjusted sales, and

$$SA = \frac{SC}{CPI\text{-}U} * 100$$

where $CPI\text{-}U$ is Consumer Price Index—Urban
SC is "hotels and motels, current gross monthly sales.

The sample calculation for the index in North Carolina travel and tourism are as follows:

Year	Taxable Sales (000)					Taxable Tourist Spending	Total Tourist Spending* to include non-taxable total = 1~5 * 1.20
	Other Retail	Restaurant/ Lodging	Food Stores	Gen'l Mdse	Gas Tax		
	(1)	(2)	(3)	(4)	(5)	(6)	(7)
1983	$202,704	$270,575	$ 90,028	$413,101	$100,000	$1,076,408	$1,291,691
1984	186,313	276,213	154,293	479,951	100,000	1,196,770	1,436,124
1985	218,393	309,608	118,294	444,434	100,000	1,190,729	1,428,875
1986	265,864	381,805	144,172	503,727	101,000	1,296,060	1,555,272
1987	288,966	408,206	140,003	551,234	90,993	1,479,402	1,775,282
1988	324,334	445,296	168,167	621,271	104,000	1,663,068	1,995,682
1989	341,096	447,042	200,831	590,669	100,000	1,679,638	2,015,566
1990	326,838	426,442	144,856	575,808	106,000	1,579,944	1,895,933

- *Column 5 for 1986-1990 is estimated based upon figures, which are the only years available at the Gas Tax Division of the State of Maine.
- Column 6 is the sum of columns 1 through 5.
- The Maine State Planning Office estimates that about 20% of all state sales is food, which is not taxable. Therefore, the taxable figures in column 6 are expanded by 20% to include tourist food sales.
- Column 3 includes only taxable items such as pet food, beer, wine, candy, etc.

Source: Sanders, et al., 1993

Table 45: Total Maine tourist spending as estimated from sales tax figures

1. Hotels and motels, current gross monthly sales ($1,000) Jan. 1981 = $23,971

2. Consumer Price Index—Urban Jan. 1981 = 260.5

3. Calculate sales adjusted for price level:

   Adjusted sales = 100 * (current sales/CPUI-U)
   = 100 * ($23,971 / 260.5)
   = $9,201.9

4. Calculate Travel Index:

   Crude index = 100 * (adjusted sales/index base)
   = 100 * (9,201.9/10,200)
   = 90.2

5. Calculate seasonally adjusted Travel Index:

   Seasonally adjusted index
   = 100 * (crude N.C. Travel Index/seasonal factor)
   = 100 * (90.2/69.5)
   =129.8

Month	Seasonal Factor
January	69.5
February	79.7
March	91.1
April	102.6
May	100.6
June	115.1
July	137.9
August	134.8
September	106.0
October	115.6
November	79.4
December	67.8

Source: Judd and Rulison, 1983

Table 46: Index of North Carolina travel and tourism, seasonal factors by X-11

The season factor was carried out using the X-11 seasonal adjustment program (SAS Institute, 1980). The example of the calculation is presented in Table 46.

Travel/Tourism Price Index (TPI)

The Travel Price Index was developed and published monthly by the U.S. Travel Data Center (USTDC, 1989) to measure the cost of the goods and services involved in the tourism industry because the U.S. travel and tourism industry includes a heterogeneous grouping of many industries. It is calculated using those components of the U.S. Consumer Price Index, which are likely to be used by the tourist. For example, food consumed in restaurants, transportation fares, and other similar goods and services related to tourism are included. Once these values have been identified, the terms composing the index are weighted by taking the ratio of each term's expenditure for the current month and dividing by the total expenditure in tourism related terms. These components are then weighted by each item's share (Backman and Uysal, 1987).

In using the Travel/Tourism Price Index, Backman and Uysal (1987) pointed that the importance of the Travel Price Index is not what it calculates but that it was the first attempt to relate travel to changing consumer costs over time. One of the strengths of U.S. T.P.I. is that it not only monitors changes in travel costs, but also can be used to assess price change impacts on tourism. However, two major problems are apparent with the index. First, use of Consumer Price Index data may result in major errors due to errors in the data in the Consumer Price Index which is compounded when used to produce the U.S. Travel Price Index. Second, the U.S. Travel Price Index does not adjust its data for seasonal variations, which are a widely discussed problem of tourism destinations.

Morley (1994) also explored the relationship between the Travel Price Index and Consumer Price Index by using the Consumer Price Index for tourism prices in demand modelling. The research detailed that in demand modelling the Consumer Price Index can be used as Travel Price Index. In Morley's study, for 10 important tourist destinations, price series for major tourist expenditure items (hotel accommodation, restaurant meals, and travel) were estimated. These tourism prices were found, with a few exceptions, to correlate very highly with the destination's CPI; the high correlations persisted even after linear time-trend effects were removed from the series (Table 47).

Moreover, in Morley's same study, detailed Australian data on tourist origins, numbers, spending breakdowns, and price changes were used to derive Tourism Price Indices for major origins of tourists to Australia. After linear time-trend effects were removed from the series, the correlation of each Tourism Price Index with the Australian CPI is very high, indicating that overall tourism prices do move very closely in accord with general consumer prices. The results confirm that it is reasonable to use CPI as a proxy for tourism prices in a demand model (Table 48).

Price Index Series	Correlation with CPI
Canada hotel	0.400
Canada restaurant	0.783
Canada travel	0.930
France hotel	0.882
France restaurant	0.946
Germany hotel	0.201
Germany restaurant	0.838
Germany travel	0.888
Italy hotel	0.984
Italy restaurant	0.990
Italy travel	0.932
Spain hotel	0.274
Spain travel	0.917
Sweden hotel	0.953
Sweden restaurant	0.848
Swiss hotel	0.031
Swiss restaurant	0.719
Turkey hotel	0.992
UK hotel	0.414
UK restaurant	0.841
UK travel	0.899
Yugoslavia hotel	1.000

*Partial correlation correcting for time-trend variable.
Source: Morley, 1994

Table 47: Tourism prices and CPI: Correlations corrected for time trend

The Australian Tourism/Travel Price Indices developed in Morley's study (1994) are generated from the International Visitor Survey (IVS) of the Bureau of Tourism Research in Australia, which reports the average expenditure of tourists on various item categories—from food, drink and accommodation, through shopping, entertainment, domestic airfares and rental cars, to gambling. There are large differences in different origins. Such differences suggest that a different price series is

Origin	Correlation
USA	0.834
Japan	0.637
New Zealand	0.687
United Kingdom	0.806
Germany	0.851
Canada	0.718

Source: Morley, 1994

Table 48: Australian tourism prices and CPI: correlations corrected for time trend

appropriate for each origin. To construct a Travel/Tourism Price Index series requires weight measures; in the International Visitor Survey (IVS), the expenditure breakdowns provide relative weights for the corresponding item categories. The breakdowns of IVS expenditure item category were straightforward with a CPI group, subgroup or expenditure class. Values of the Australian Travel/Tourism Price Indices for the period 1972 to 1991 are presented in Table 49.

MISCELLANEOUS INDICES

There are a variety of Miscellaneous Indices that explore other different travel and tourism measures developed for a variety of specific purposes. The demographic index was developed by Huan (1997) to measure and monitor the demographic backgrounds of U.S. Great Lakes region overnight pleasure travel parties in Ontario, Canada. The loyalty index was constructed by Coopers & Lybrand Consulting (1996) for the Canadian Tourism Commission to determine the switching potential of Canadians travelling to Canada or the U.S. The National Tourism Indicators were developed by Statistics Canada to portray the evolution of tourism in Canada on a quarterly basis, and included are the estimates of supply and demand for each of the main commodities and employment for tourism industries (Statistics Canada, 1996a).

The Peaking Index is a measure that summarizes data on temporal-use levels into a single value (Stynes, 1978). The Service Index was developed by Huan (1997) to measure and monitor the rating of Canadian services in comparison to home country services of U.S. travelers. The Tourism Attractiveness Index was used as the

	Origin					
Year	U.S.A.	Japan	Zealand	Kingdom	Germany	Canada
1972	25.24	26.40	27.05	26.02	25.21	25.45
1973	43.70	43.91	44.87	44.45	44.01	44.12
1974	50.61	50.51	51.37	50.95	50.50	50.61
1975	59.90	57.36	58.01	57.43	57.04	57.16
1976	64.73	65.22	65.83	65.19	64.65	64.92
1977	71.86	72.97	73.31	72.31	71.59	71.85
1978	78.35	79.46	79.81	78.82	78.13	78.33
1979	89.66	90.91	89.01	89.38	87.44	89.09
1980	100.00	100.00	100.00	100.00	100.00	100.00
1981	110.30	114.27	108.93	108.26	110.34	110.42
1982	122.05	121.74	121.66	121.87	121.90	122.16
1983	133.98	135.42	133.66	134.09	134.18	134.73
1984	140.87	142.78	143.63	141.09	141.80	142.12
1985	153.43	154.34	152.12	152.29	153.47	152.63
1986	165.04	165.66	164.75	166.02	165.65	166.16
1987	176.93	177.20	177.00	176.69	176.78	177.07
1988	191.77	180.57	188.53	193.09	189.92	191.41
1989	207.52	200.50	206.70	210.72	209.64	210.50
1990	216.89	206.20	202.31	213.68	216.80	210.47
1991	220.07	234.87	222.07	220.31	223.75	217.26

Source: Morley, 1994

Table 49: Tourism price indices for international tourists in Australia by origin

measurement of the potential of candidate regions for attracting tourists (Gearing, Swart, and Var, 1974). The Tourism Climatic Index is a composite measure of the climatic well-being of tourists and also provides a second, indirect benefit, in that it may help to promote better use of climatic resources in various parts of the world (Mieczkowski, 1985).

The travel dispersal index can be used as a tourist typology. Tourists are classified along a scale from inactive to very active in terms of spatial behavior, where the latter have the highest interest in the visited country (Oppermann, 1992a). It has also been employed by the National Tourism Department to identify those markets whose spatial patterns conform the most with the goals of national tourism policy. All the original ideas, technical formulas, statistical outputs, and applications of the indices in this Miscellaneous Indices group will be detailed in the following part of this section.

Demographic Index

The demographic index was developed by Huan (1997) to measure and monitor the demographic backgrounds of U.S. Great Lakes region overnight pleasure travel parties in Ontario, Canada. In the study, the data were collected by Statistics Canada as part of the International Travel Survey (for travel parties coming to Canada from other countries). The demographic index including male and female age groups is defined as follows:

$$\text{Fe/Male Index: } \frac{\text{\# of fe/male (0-19; 20-34; 35-54; 55+)}}{\text{\# of the travel party}} * 100$$

These male and female indices show the importance levels (proportion) of all U.S. travel party age groups. In Tables 50 and 51, and Figures 16 and 17, the Male and Female Indices show that adult males and adult females aged 35 to 54 from the U.S. Great Lakes states were the largest and the most important visiting groups in Ontario, Canada, especially in the winter seasons. Senior males and senior females aged 55 or over were the second most important group to visit Canada. The change patterns of their indices were similar, which may mean that senior males and senior females tended to travel together. The age groups (male and female) from 20 to 34 were the third most important travel age group. The importance level of each age group for a travel party is different and changes over time.

Loyalty Index

To determine the switching potential of Canadians travelling to Canada or the U.S., a loyalty index was constructed by Coopers & Lybrand Consulting (1996) for the Canadian Tourism Commission. The loyalty was based upon three questions pertaining to the longest trip of the season in the past years:

1. How interested are you in taking a similar trip to this destination in the next two years? (Q6b)
2. How interested are you in taking a similar trip to the United States in the next two years? (Q6c)
3. How interested are you in taking a similar trip to Canada in the next two years? (Q6e)

The index was constructed using simple arithmetic. For those who travelled in Canada, their loyalty index score (I) was:

$$I = Q6b - Q6c$$

Likewise, for those who travelled in the U.S., their loyalty index score was:

$$I = Q6b - Q6e$$

The rationale is that someone who travelled to Canada and who is very interested in taking a trip to the same destination (i.e., within Canada), but not at all interested in taking a similar trip to the U.S., would be a "loyal Canadian traveller" (and not likely to switch to the U.S.). In this case their score on Q6b would be "very interested" or 4, and Q6c would be "not at all interested" or 1:

$$I = Q6b - Q6c = 4 - 1 = 3$$

On the other hand, a "potential switcher to the U.S." would be someone who had travelled in Canada and who is not very interested in taking a trip to the same

Age:	Male Index 0–19	20–34	35–54	55+
1990 Jan–Mar	6.64	15.07	19.98	5.05
1990 Apr–Jun	6.99	8.55	19.83	15.98
1990 Jul-Sep	11.90	7.79	18.21	10.91
1990 Oct–Dec	7.84	9.59	18.87	12.29
1991 Jan–Mar	2.98	11.44	14.02	16.01
1991 Apr–Jun	5.77	13.81	19.24	14.14
1991 Jul-Sep	11.47	7.32	20.80	10.48
1991 Oct-Dec	4.29	7.33	18.44	14.98
1992 Jan–Mar	4.75	15.09	21.36	3.73
1992 Apr–Jun	6.05	11.43	15.00	13.97
1992 Jul-Sep	11.02	6.26	20.72	12.90
1992 Oct-Dec	3.94	8.78	16.98	13.50
1993 Jan–Mar	4.57	13.91	18.02	9.39
1993 Apr–Jun	6.62	8.00	19.23	18.34
1993 Jul-Sep	9.19	8.24	17.36	13.64
1993 Oct-Dec	4.37	9.26	15.32	15.58
1994 Jan–Mar	9.63	7.20	18.09	11.07
1994 Apr–Jun	5.46	7.77	19.83	19.98
1994 Jul-Sep	10.35	8.38	17.73	12.71
1994 Oct-Dec	7.29	8.24	12.44	13.90
1995 Jan–Mar	8.75	9.23	20.06	10.23
1995 Apr–Jun	6.71	9.70	17.51	17.97
1995 Jul-Sep	10.35	8.32	17.52	11.97
1995 Oct–Dec	7.52	10.28	12.46	13.62

Male/age groups

1. 0–19: Young
2. 20–34: Adult
3. 35–54: Middle age
4. 55+: Senior

Source: Huan, 1997

Table 50: Male index of U.S. Great Lakes region travellers in Ontario

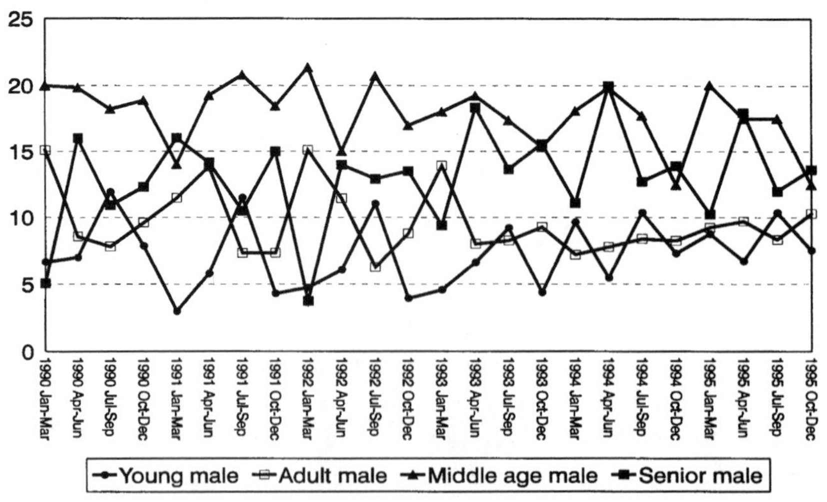

Source: Huan, 1997

Figure 16: Male index of U.S. Great Lakes region travellers in Ontario

	Female Index			
Age:	0–19	20–34	35–54	55+
1990 Jan–Mar	8.64	14.46	19.48	10.68
1990 Apr–Jun	5.54	10.59	16.68	15.84
1990 Jul-Sep	10.84	10.25	18.39	11.70
1990 Oct-Dec	5.75	9.27	23.06	13.33
1991 Jan–Mar	5.40	12.71	23.30	14.13
1991 Apr–Jun	5.37	8.47	19.37	13.82
1991 Jul-Sep	11.46	7.74	20.65	10.07
1991 Oct-Dec	7.72	13.71	17.41	16.12
1992 Jan–Mar	8.05	19.11	23.81	4.10
1992 Apr–Jun	7.41	14.36	16.70	15.07
1992 Jul-Sep	10.57	6.86	19.29	12.39
1992 Oct-Dec	7.39	14.41	18.17	16.84
1993 Jan–Mar	3.39	17.83	21.77	11.12
1993 Apr–Jun	6.02	9.32	18.08	14.40
1993 Jul-Sep	11.62	7.64	18.34	13.98
1993 Oct-Dec	7.35	13.18	17.98	16.97
1994 Jan–Mar	5.22	14.23	23.73	10.84
1994 Apr–Jun	5.16	9.44	18.08	14.27
1994 Jul-Sep	9.49	7.50	20.55	13.29
1994 Oct-Dec	8.40	12.05	20.18	17.50
1995 Jan–Mar	6.91	12.99	23.26	8.57
1995 Apr–Jun	5.35	10.53	16.49	15.75
1995 Jul-Sep	12.74	8.05	19.08	11.97
1995 Oct-Dec	7.70	10.20	20.76	17.46

Female/age group

1. 0–19: Young
2. 20–34: Adult
3. 35–54: Middle age
4. 55+: Senior

Source: Huan, 1997

Table 51: Female index of U.S. Great Lakes region travellers in Ontario

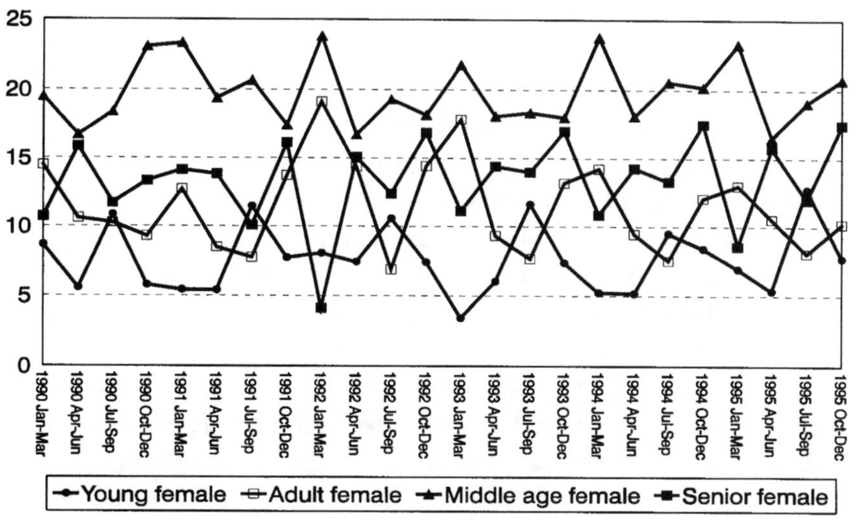

Source: Huan, 1997

Figure 17: Female index of U.S. Great Lakes region travellers in Ontario

destination (i.e., within Canada) (Q6b = 1), but is very interested in taking a trip to the U.S. (Q6c = 4), or:

I = Q6b - Q6c = 1 - 4 = -3

In this way, a loyalty index was created, with values ranging from -3 to +3 for both travellers to the U.S. and Canada. The distribution of index scores for both groups is shown in Table 52. As may be seen from the table, the loyalty index defines four groups of travellers, based on where they travelled in the past and their relative interest in visiting the U.S. and Canada in the future:

1. Potential Switchers to Canada: Those who took their longest trip of the season in the past year to the U.S., but have an equal or greater interest in travelling to Canada than to the U.S. in the future. They were seen as a key group that represented an excellent opportunity for Canada to incrementally increase the amount of domestic travel.
2. Potential Switchers to the U.S.: Those who took their longest trip of the season in the past year to Canada, but their interest in the U.S. is as strong or stronger than their interest in Canada in terms of future travel. They are also a key group, but one that represents a potential threat for Canada, since these travellers have a high propensity to switch their domestic trips to U.S. destinations instead.
3. Loyal Canadian Travellers: Those who travelled in Canada and have little interest in taking similar trips across the border.
4. Loyal U.S. Travellers: Those who travelled in the U.S. and have little desire to switch to Canada.

National Tourism Indicators (NTI)

The National Tourism Indicators (Statistics Canada, 1996a) were developed by Statistics Canada in 1996. The indicators portray the evolution of tourism in Canada on a quarterly basis. Estimates of supply and demand for each of the main commodities and employment for tourism industries as identified in the 1988 Tourism Satellite Account (TSA) are recorded as time series. All series are benchmarked to the 1988 TSA.

The quarterly NTI exists in two versions, one unadjusted and the other adjusted for seasonal variation. Most seasonal adjustment in Statistics Canada is undertaken using X-11-ARIMA. The X11 method involves the application of moving averages to estimate the trendcycle, seasonal, and irregular components of the series, with special treatment for outliers and foreseeable trading-days. The advantages of X-11-ARIMA are twofold. First, by carrying out the seasonal adjustment at the most detailed level, seasonal shifts in the aggregates are more easily explained. Second, the calculation of seasonally adjusted aggregates by summation preserves the accounting identified in the system. This is much more convenient for users.

The National Tourism Indicators contain five categories: (1) supply, the production in Canada of the specified commodity; (2) tourism demand in Canada, the domestic demand plus exports and thus represents total demand by visitors for Canadian produced good and services; (3) tourism domestic demand; (4) tourism exports, the spending by Canadian residents, on the specified commodity, as a result of tourism; and (5) employment, corresponding to the "person at work" concept which is close to the concept of "person-year," in that it contains adjustments for the number of months worked. The results of the Canadian National Tourism Indicators (seasonally adjusted/ unadjusted) are presented in Appendix B.

Peaking Index

The Peaking Index is a measure that summarizes a substantial amount of data on temporal-use levels into a single value (Stynes, 1978). This measure is an open-ended scale with a minimum value of 0.00. The greater the degree of concentration (peak use), the greater the value of the index. The Peaking Index is derived from a graph called an *excedence curve*—so called because the curve illustrates the number of times a particular use level was reached or exceeded.

For example, the number of visitors at many tourism businesses varies dramatically over time (Smith, 1995). Restaurants boom on weekends and holidays, but are quiet in the early part of the week. Resorts are booked solid for a few weeks or months and then operate at a much reduced level for the rest of the year—or may even close. It can be helpful for a business planner or recreation programmer to be able to measure quantitatively the tendency of people to use a facility or visit a destination in one time period as opposed to other time periods. The Peaking Index summarizes the data and provides a succinct measure. The formula for the Peaking Index is:

$$P_n = \frac{V_1 - V_n}{(n - 1)\, V_1} * 100$$

where P_n is the Peaking Index,
V_1 is the number of visitors during the business period,
V_n is the number of visitors during the nth period,
n is the reference period (1 = business period).

		Travelled to Canada (n=1, 975)	Travelled to U.S. (N=366)
Potential	-3	1%	2%
Switcher to	-2	2%	5%
the other	-1	8%	15%
Country	0	38%	43%
Loyal	1	22%	15%
Traveller	2	17%	10%
	3	12%	9%

Source: Coopers & Lybrand Consulting, 1996

Table 52: Distribution of loyalty index scores

The value of the Peaking Index depends not only on the degree of peaking but also on the total volume of business and on the choice of time periods used for analysis (Smith, 1995). The index will be changed if the chosen time period changes from day to week, or to another appropriate time period. The data should cover a reasonably long time period, often an entire season or year for useful comparison. The use of the Peaking Index is for comparison between businesses or for examination of trends in peaking over time in one facility.

Table 53 provides an example of the calculation of P_n. In this case (Smith, 1995), the occupancy rates are for hotels in Vancouver, British Columbia. The busiest month in Vancouver is traditionally August, with an average occupancy rate of 96 per cent. This drops off until a low is reached in December. A value of 6 for *n*, reflecting the midpoint in the number of months over a year, was chosen. Application of the formula produced a value of 2.90 for P_n.

Service Rating Index

The Service Index was developed by Huan (1997) to measure and monitor the rating of Canadian services in comparison to home country services. In the study, the data were collected by Statistics Canada through the International Travel Survey looking at travel parties from other countries. The Service Index for different types of ratings of services was defined as follows:

Service Index => better: same: not as good => 1: 2: 3 => 100: 50: 0

*The Service Index could be for (1) transportation, (2) accommodation, (3) hospitality, (4) value of money, (5) variety of things to do/see in Canada)

These Service Indices show the different ratings of services by travellers. In Table 54 and Figure 18, most travellers reflected that "Hospitality," "Transporta-

Month	Occupancy rate (%)
August	96
July	91
September	91
June	89
October	85
May	82
April	74
March	72
November	70
February	60
January	53
December	49

Source: Smith, 1995

Table 53: Hotel occupancy rates for Vancouver, Canada

	Service Index 1	2	3	4	5
1990 Jan–Mar	66.68	51.07	66.56	46.70	62.18
1990 Apr–Jun	61.71	54.51	66.74	39.23	63.35
1990 Jul-Sep	57.81	52.97	65.86	33.77	60.11
1990 Oct-Dec	68.25	53.97	67.77	39.81	63.96
1991 Jan–Mar	66.05	51.79	65.91	30.82	62.05
1991 Apr–Jun	58.48	49.20	62.68	22.55	55.08
1991 Jul-Sep	60.86	50.93	66.94	18.71	58.34
1991 Oct-Dec	71.26	54.66	64.95	24.95	65.98
1992 Jan–Mar	68.98	58.25	55.10	50.52	59.74
1992 Apr–Jun	64.50	53.83	68.81	32.28	61.81
1992 Jul-Sep	61.07	51.47	64.39	25.30	59.78
1992 Oct-Dec	67.49	53.30	65.49	32.93	64.51
1993 Jan–Mar	71.03	57.85	68.28	39.39	64.61
1993 Apr–Jun	61.18	51.00	64.39	38.59	59.89
1993 Jul-Sep	60.41	50.70	66.67	38.76	62.05
1993 Oct-Dec	66.86	51.37	59.83	38.28	67.80
1994 Jan–Mar	67.86	55.87	68.75	43.43	63.91
1994 Apr–Jun	66.77	53.21	66.95	46.62	60.48
1994 Jul-Sep	58.47	50.51	66.47	52.67	62.77
1994 Oct-Dec	65.16	57.93	68.83	56.42	70.29
1995 Jan–Mar	68.74	55.82	66.35	51.86	64.70
1995 Apr–Jun	62.69	50.47	65.26	48.76	59.42
1995 Jul-Sep	57.14	51.45	66.91	52.07	61.58
1995 Oct-Dec	61.94	57.76	70.45	58.40	68.40

Services

1. Transportation
2. Accommodation
3. Hospitality
4. Value of money
5. Variety of things to do and see

Source: Huan, 1997

Table 54: Service rating index of U.S. Great Lakes region travellers in Ontario

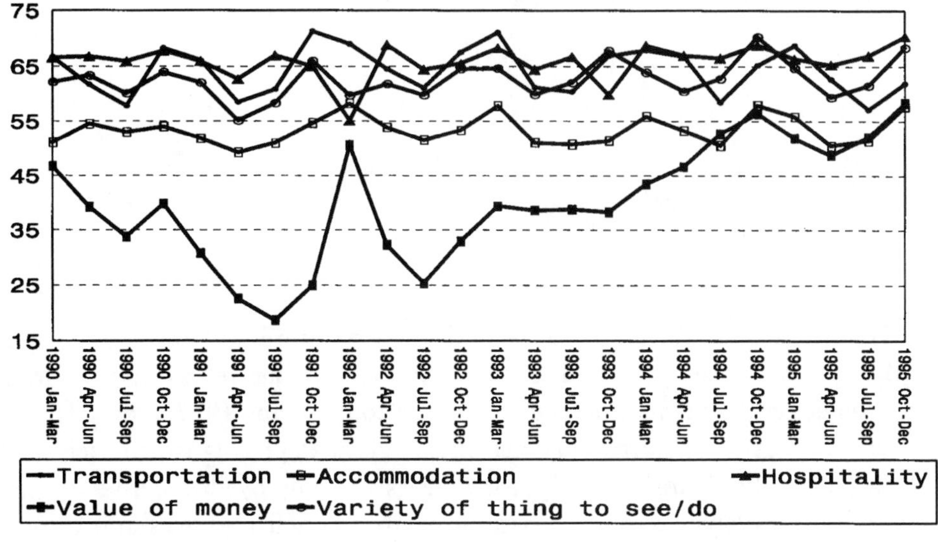

Source: Huan, 1997

Figure 18: Service rating index of U.S. Great Lakes region travellers in Ontario

tion," and "Varieties of Things to Do and See" were the top three services that were better in Canada than in the U.S.A. From these travellers' responses, the services of "Accommodation" were almost the same in Canada as in the U.S.A. Moreover, since summer 1992 (from July to September), more travellers thought that the value for their money was improving in Canada. In the following summers, the travellers thought that the value for their money continued to improve in Canada compared to the U.S.

Tourism Attractiveness Index

In 1974, Gearing, Swart, and Var (1974) defined the Tourism Attractiveness Index as the measurement of the potential of candidate regions for attracting tourists. Moreover, Gearing, Swart, and Var (1974) also provided a review of the evolution of the Tourism Attractiveness Index.

Clawson and Knetsch (1963) were the first to suggest the possibility of developing specific and objective rating scales to measure the attractiveness of outdoor recreation areas. Ellis (1965), working on the similar problem, designed a model based on systems theory; he tried to describe and analyze the socioeconomic system using physical system concepts. In this widely referenced work, Ellis uses a model which can be thought of as an electrical analog where origins act like sources of current, in this case, for campers. The current follows various paths of different resistances and distributes itself in the system in a way to achieve minimization of energy. Therefore, the flow to each park is a function of resistances of the parks, available linkages, and the current strength at the origins. The formula is as follows:

$$F_j = A_j P_j$$

where F_j is the flow of camper-days enter park, j, in one season
A_j is the attraction index
P_j is the pressure of user demand at the park gate.

Moreover, the flow through any link is given by:

$$R_k = C(TD_k)^b$$

where C is a constant for all links,
TD_k is the time to traverse link k,
b is a constant exponent.

Following Ellis, Van Doren (1967) devised a Camping Attractiveness Index for Michigan state parks. His index is based on 55 variables related to (1) outdoor recreation activities, (2) natural environment resources, and (3) camping facilities and services. Rather subjectively, determined values were assigned to each of the variables selected by Van Doren. Factor analysis was employed to derive aggregate scores for the variables related to natural environmental resources and camping facilities and services. The Camping Attractiveness Index of a park was a weighted combination of its scores on the individual variables. By using the same method,

Auger (1974) also attempted to determine attractiveness indices for campgrounds in Quebec by using 46 variables grouped in four categories, i.e., natural characteristics, water, services, and activities. By assigning different scales to these characteristics, Auger was able to rank campgrounds in Quebec in term of attractiveness.

Cesario, Goldstone, and Knetsch (1969) also suggested another formulation of the attractiveness index. This simply considers the type, quantity, and quality of facilities offered and is defined as a sum of products. The utility of having an activity and the quality of activity are multiplied, and this product is added for a set of activities. Therefore, this attractiveness measurement may be more convenient in analysis where only limited data are available.

Cheung (1972) tried to develop an attractiveness index that give insights into the structure of relations that determine participation at a given park which is part of a system. The attractiveness is expressed as a function of the physical characteristics of the facilities and the services offered at a site. The analysis considered a set of 12 provincial and national parks. The attractiveness indices of the twelve parks are presented in Table 55 and the formula is:

$$T_j = S\Sigma\, S_e\, \Sigma\, R_m Q_m\, ,\ j = 1, \ldots, 12$$

where T_j = attractiveness of park j,
S_e = relative popularity rating of activity e,
R_m = relative importance rating of facility m, and
Q_m = score of facility m, according to its quantity and quality

Cesario (1973) also considered park attractiveness, population center emissiveness, and the effect of distance in outdoor recreation travel and found camping attractiveness indexes for 46 Ontario population centers. In a joint article, Cesario and Knestch suggested the following model:

Park	Attractiveness T_j
Buffalo Pound	96.12
Cypress Hill	45.26
Duck Mountain	126.40
Echo Valley	112.05
Good Spirit	76.56
Green Water	61.46
Prince Albert	88.75
Moose Mountain	113.11
Pike Lake	96.10
Rowan's Ravine	59.01
Battleford's	104.28
Besant	26.60

Source: Cheung, 1972

Table 55: Attractiveness ratings of the selected Canadian parks

$$Vij = g[Xi, Yj, f(cij)],\ j = 1, \ldots, 12$$

where *Vij* = the number of visits per unit time made to site *j* from population center *i*;

Xi = a measure of the combined effects on recreation trip-making of certain characteristics of population center (e.g., population size, median income, etc.);

Yj = a measure of combined effects on recreation trip-making of certain characteristics of recreation site *j* (e.g., land and/or water acreage, parking spaces, etc.; and

cij = the generalized cost of travel from *i* to *j* (e.g. road mileage, travel time, out-of-pocket expenses, or some combination of all these indicators).

Gearing, Swart, and Var (1974) established a measure of touristic attractiveness for the Turkish Ministry of Tourism. A set of 17 criteria were selected, with attention to their "independence," which are the principle measures for the determination of "touristic attractiveness." Then, through a process designed to elicit consistent judgements from an interviewee, the contributions of 26 tourism "experts" were combined to form a set of numerical weights which establish the relative importance of the 17 criteria.

The weighting methodology was developed by Churchman and Ackoff (1957) but with some modification to take advantage of the hierarchical structure of the criteria being used (see Appendix C). The criteria weights and implied ranks of a representative interviewee and the average of 26 experts are presented in Table 56 for a hypothetical site. For computing a weighted total for the hypothetical touristic area, the weights in Table 57 should be employed. This score allows a comparison to be made between any two touristic areas, and a ranking of all the 65 can be established on the basis of their respective scores (see Table 58).

Var, Beck, and Loftus (1977) employed the same methodology Gearing, Swart, and Var (1974) had used and tried to explore the determination of touristic attractiveness of the tourism areas in British Columbia. They defined the formula of touristic attractiveness of a district or region (j) as follows:

$$T_j = f(N_j, S_j, H_j, R_j, I_j)$$

where T_j = touristic attractiveness
N_j = natural factors
S_j = social factors
H_j = historical factors
R_j = recreation and shopping opportunities
I_j = accessibility and accommodation above minimum touristic quality

Tourism Climatic Index (TCI)

The Tourism Climatic Index is a composite measure of the climatic well-being of tourists (Mieczkowski, 1985). TCIs also provide a second, indirect benefit, in that they may help to promote better use of climatic resources in various parts of the world. This is especially important for the developing countries that have en-

Criteria	Representative Interviewee Weight (W_j)	Rank (r)	Average of 26 experts Weight (W_j)	Rank (r)	Expected Rank Sum (E)[a]	Actual Rank Sum (S_j)[a]	(S-Ej)a
1	0.177	2	0.132	1	234.0	93.0	-141.0
2	0.053	7	0.099	4	234.0	124.5	-109.5
3	0.031	9	0.051	9	234.0	206.0	- 28.0
4	0.004	16	0.029	14	234.0	358.5	124.5
5	0.016	12.5	0.026	15	234.0	310.5	76.5
6	0.000	17	0.011	17	234.0	400.5	166.5
7	0.010	15	0.054	7	234.0	243.0	9.0
8	0.076	5	0.057	6	234.0	207.5	- 26.5
9	0.110	4	0.053	8	234.0	217.0	- 17.0
10	0.044	8	0.065	5	234.0	183.0	- 51.0
11	0.075	6	0.046	10	234.0	232.0	- 2.0
12	0.016	12.5	0.015	16	234.0	382.0	148.0
13	0.022	11	0.032	13	234.0	289.0	55.0
14	0.030	10	0.045	11	234.0	268.5	34.5
15	0.016	12.5	0.036	12	234.0	282.5	48.5
16	0.179	1	0.131	2	234.0	78.0	-156.0
17	0.141	3	0.125	3	234.0	107.5	-126.5

Source: Gearing, Swart, and Var, 1974

Table 56: Criteria weights and implied ranks of a representative interviewee and the average of 26 experts

Criterion	Weight	Evaluation
1. Natural beauty	0.132	0.80
2. Climate	0.099	0.70
3. Artistic and architectural features	0.051	0.70
4. Folk festival	0.029	0.70
5. Distinctive local feature	0.026	0.60
6. Fairs and exhibits	0.011	0.60
7. Attitudes toward tourists	0.054	0.60
8. Ancient ruins	0.057	0.70
9. Religious significance	0.053	0.50
10. Historical prominence	0.065	0.70
11. Sports facilities	0.046	0.30
12. Educational facilities	0.032	0.40
13. Resting and tranquility	0.032	0.40
14. Nighttime reaction	0.045	0.30
15. Shopping	0.036	0.60
16. Infrastructure above m.t.p.	0.131	0.70
17. Food and lodging above m.t.p.	0.125	0.70
Weight total ("score")		0.90280

Source: Gearing, Swart, and Var, 1974

Table 57: Evaluation and weight of a tourist area

Touristic Areas	Score
IZMIR	924.78
ISTANBUL	906.00
ANTALYA	764.80
BURSA	760.15
AYDIN	710.65
ANKARA	686.72
KAYSERI	681.93
FINIKE	665.92
ESKISEHIR-KUTAHYA	656.92
MANAVGAT-SIDE	645.00
MERSIN	637.25
KOCAELI-SAKARYA	630.35
NEVSEHIR	625.00
KONYA	564.85

Source: Gearing, Swart, and Var, 1974

Table 58: Ranking of the touristic areas in decreasing order of touristic attractiveness

tered the international tourist market. The classification scheme for mapping TCIs is presented in Table 59 and its formula is as follows:

$$TCI = 4cid + cia + 2R + 2S + W$$

where *cid* is daytime comfort index, composed of T1 = maximum daily DBT (dry bulb temperature) and RHmin = minimum daily RH (Relative humidity),
cia is daily comfort index, composed of T2 = mean daily DBT (dry bulb temperature) and RHa = mean daily RH (Relative humidity),
R is precipitation in mm of rain,
S is daily hours of bright sunshine,
W is wind speed in m/s or km/h.

Travel Dispersal Index

The travel dispersal index was developed by Oppermann (1992b). Unlike a Trip Index analyzing only one aspect of the tourists' intranational travel behavior, the travel dispersal index (TDI) integrates five variables of the intranational travel behavior in a comprehensive analysis. These five variables are (1) length of stay in the country, (2) number of overnight destinations, (3) number of different types of accommodation, (4) number of different types of transportation used, and (5) number of different types of travel organization.

The application of the TDI is twofold. On one side, the travel dispersal index can be used as a tourist typology in which the tourists are classified along a scale from inactive to very active in terms of spatial behavior, where the latter have the highest interest in the visited country. On the other hand, the travel dispersal index can be applied as a market segmentation tool by national tourism departments to

Numeric Value of Indices	Code	Descriptive Category	Mapping Category
90–100	9	Ideal	Excellent
80–89	8	Excellent	
70–79	7	Very good	Very good & good
60–69	6	Good	
50–59	5	Acceptable	Acceptable
40–49	4	Marginal	
30–39	3	Unfavourable	Unfavourable
20–29	2	Very unfavourable	
10–19	1	Extremely unfavourable	
9--9	0	Impossible	
-10--10	-1	Impossible	

Source: Mieczkowski, 1985

Table 59: The classification scheme for mapping TCIs

identify those markets whose spatial patterns conform the most with the goals of national tourism policy. The formula of travel dispersal index developed by Oppermann (1992) is:

$$TDI = LS + OD + A + T + TO \quad \text{(weighted)}$$

where *LS* is the length of stay in the country,
OD is the number of overnight destinations,
A is the number of different types of accommodation,
T is the number of different types of transportation used,
TO is the number of different types of travel organization.

The parameters of the travel dispersal for weighting the ingredients (five independent variables in the above formula) of travel dispersal index are presented in Table 60. Some of the results of a study conducted by Oppermann (1992) are detailed in Table 61.

Parameter		Weighting (in Points) 0	1	2	3	4	5
OD	Number of overnight destinations	0	1	2	3–5	6–10	> 10
LS	Number of nights	0	1–3	4–7	8–14	> 14	
A	Number of different types of accommodation	0	1	> 1			
T	Number of different types of transportation	0	1	> 1			
TO	Travel organization:						
	Package		X				
	Individual			X			

Source: Oppermann, 1992b

Table 60: Parameters of Travel Dispersal

Variable	Travel Dispersal Index 4–6 (Less Active)	7–9	10–12	13–15 (More Active)
N =	251	117	39	32
Individual travellers (in %)	45.0	50.4	74.4	96.9
Sex				
Percentage of females	38.6	42.7	46.2	46.9
Repeat visitors (in %)	38.6	38.5	33.3	6.2
Degree of concentration (in % of nights in Malaysia)				
Kuala Lumpur	37.4	38.2	26.7	14.0
Penang	41.3	35.8	21.6	16.4
Kuala Lumpur & Penang	78.6	74.0	48.2	30.5
Average length of stay in Malaysia (in nights)	3.5	8.2	13.1	28.9
Number of overnight destinations	1.1	2.2	3.5	8.2

Source: Oppermann, 1992b

Table 61: Tourist characteristics by Travel Dispersal Index

CONCLUSION

We noted that indices have been widely used in scientific research. But the examples also show another picture as well. The different indices offer several practical management advantages to measure and compare a state or regional tourist activity, to assist in setting standards, for calculations which quickly show tourists' spending in terms of a constant value, and for planning and projection. The five major groups employed here include: (1) Hotel/Restaurant Indices, (2) Activity/Trip Indices, (3) Geographical/Population Indices, (4) Price/Economic Indices, and (5) Miscellaneous Indices. Depending on the situation the manager, planner, or researcher encounters, the information should provide the basis for formulating an index, or provide for the design of a variation to address the specific need.

There are several important issues that have an impact on the use of these measures. First, it is very important that when we build an index that will be used to compare one situation to another, the basis upon which the data are collected in each case must be clearly understood. We might find that the sampling frame was changed, and we chose to look only at tall people rather than tall and short travelers. Or if we are inquiring about total expenditures, then we want to be certain the values being reported include the same ingredients. If an index measure is higher or lower, then we must be certain the comparison is "apples to apples."

For example, some continuous national surveys have been done as additions to other ongoing surveys that have nothing to do with travel. Certain results emerge. But in a few instances, the survey gathering procedures are changed, allowing the survey to be done independently or as a stand-alone effort (e.g., a computer-aided telephone interview). Some evidence suggests that the relative proportion of some events changes. If we were evaluating the relative impact of our activities, this methodological artifact could pose a problem in interpreting the outcome.

The volume of data will also be important to think about when we consider how valuable an index can be. As we expand the amount of data being available in tourism and hospitality, "data mining" will grow. With attempts to improve information and knowledge in the industry, measures like the indices described here will become useful barometers for understanding growth, decline, relative abundance and performance. While many of the measures described here will prove useful, other creative managers will develop even more effective tools.

Appendix A

Consumer Price Index

Historical Consumer Price Index for All Urban Consumers (CPI-U): U. S. city average, all items

(1982–84 = 100, unless otherwise noted)

Year	Jan.	Feb.	Mar.	Apr.	May	June	July	Aug.	Sep.	Oct.	Nov.	Dec.	Semiannual Averages 1st Half	Semiannual Averages 2nd half	Annual Avg.	% Change from Previous Dec.	% Change from Previous Annual Avg.
1913	9.8	9.8	9.8	9.8	9.7	9.8	9.9	9.9	10.0	10.0	10.1	10.0			9.9		
1914	10.0	9.9	9.9	9.8	9.9	9.9	10.0	10.2	10.2	10.1	10.2	10.1			10.0	1.0	1.0
1915	10.1	10.0	9.9	10.0	10.1	10.1	10.1	10.1	10.1	10.2	10.3	10.3			10.1	2.0	1.0
1916	10.4	10.4	10.5	10.6	10.7	10.8	10.8	10.9	11.1	11.3	11.5	11.6			10.9	12.6	7.9
1917	11.7	12.0	12.0	12.6	12.8	13.0	12.8	13.0	13.3	13.5	13.5	13.7			12.8	18.1	17.4
1918	14.0	14.1	14.0	14.2	14.5	14.7	15.1	15.4	15.7	16.0	16.3	16.5			15.1	20.4	18.0
1919	16.5	16.2	16.4	16.7	16.9	16.9	17.4	17.7	17.8	18.1	18.5	18.9			17.3	14.5	14.6
1920	19.3	19.5	19.7	20.3	20.6	20.9	20.8	20.3	20.0	19.9	19.8	19.4			20.0	2.6	15.6
1921	19.0	18.4	18.3	18.1	17.7	17.6	17.7	17.7	17.5	17.5	17.4	17.3			17.9	-10.8	-10.5
1922	16.9	16.9	16.7	16.7	16.7	16.7	16.8	16.6	16.6	16.7	16.8	16.9			16.8	-2.3	-6.1
1923	16.8	16.8	16.8	16.9	16.9	17.0	17.2	17.1	17.2	17.3	17.3	17.3			17.1	2.4	1.8
1924	17.3	17.2	17.1	17.0	17.0	17.0	17.1	17.0	17.1	17.2	17.2	17.3			17.1	.0	.0
1925	17.3	17.2	17.3	17.2	17.3	17.5	17.7	17.7	17.7	17.7	18.0	17.9			17.5	3.5	2.3
1926	17.9	17.9	17.8	17.9	17.8	17.7	17.5	17.4	17.5	17.6	17.7	17.7			17.7	-1.1	1.1
1927	17.5	17.4	17.3	17.3	17.4	17.6	17.3	17.2	17.3	17.4	17.3	17.3			17.4	-2.3	-1.7
1928	17.3	17.1	17.1	17.1	17.2	17.1	17.1	17.1	17.3	17.2	17.2	17.1			17.1	-1.2	-1.7
1929	17.1	17.1	17.0	16.9	17.0	17.1	17.3	17.3	17.3	17.3	17.3	17.2			17.1	.6	.0
1930	17.1	17.0	16.9	17.0	16.9	16.8	16.6	16.5	16.6	16.5	16.4	16.1			16.7	-6.4	-2.3
1931	15.9	15.7	15.6	15.5	15.3	15.1	15.1	15.1	15.0	14.9	14.7	14.6			15.2	-9.3	-9.0
1932	14.3	14.1	14.0	13.9	13.7	13.6	13.6	13.5	13.4	13.3	13.2	13.1			13.7	-10.3	-9.9
1933	12.9	12.7	12.6	12.6	12.6	12.7	13.1	13.2	13.2	13.2	13.2	13.2			13.0	.8	-5.1
1934	13.2	13.3	13.3	13.3	13.3	13.4	13.4	13.4	13.6	13.5	13.5	13.4			13.4	1.5	3.1

Year	Jan.	Feb.	Mar.	Apr.	May	June	July	Aug.	Sep.	Oct.	Nov.	Dec.	Semiannual Averages		Annual	% Change From Previous	
													1st Half	2nd half	Avg.	Dec.	Annual Avg.
1935	13.6	13.7	13.7	13.8	13.8	13.7	13.7	13.7	13.7	13.7	13.8	13.8			13.7	3.0	2.2
1936	13.8	13.8	13.7	13.7	13.7	13.8	13.9	14.0	14.0	14.0	14.0	14.0			13.9	1.4	1.5
1937	14.1	14.1	14.2	14.3	14.4	14.4	14.5	14.5	14.6	14.6	14.5	14.4			14.4	2.9	3.6
1938	14.2	14.1	14.1	14.2	14.1	14.1	14.1	14.1	14.1	14.0	14.0	14.0			14.1	-2.8	-2.1
1939	14.0	13.9	13.9	13.8	13.8	13.8	13.8	13.8	14.1	14.0	14.0	14.0			13.9	.0	-1.4
1940	13.9	14.0	14.0	14.0	14.0	14.1	14.0	14.0	14.0	14.0	14.0	14.1			14.0	.7	.7
1941	14.1	14.1	14.2	14.3	14.4	14.7	14.7	14.9	15.1	15.3	15.4	15.5			14.7	9.9	5.0
1942	15.7	15.8	16.0	16.1	16.3	16.3	16.4	16.5	16.5	16.7	16.8	16.9			16.3	9.0	10.9
1943	16.9	16.9	17.2	17.4	17.5	17.5	17.4	17.3	17.4	17.4	17.4	17.4			17.3	3.0	6.1
1944	17.4	17.4	17.4	17.5	17.5	17.6	17.7	17.7	17.7	17.7	17.7	17.8			17.6	2.3	1.7
1945	17.8	17.8	17.8	17.8	17.9	18.1	18.1	18.1	18.1	18.1	18.1	18.2			18.0	2.2	2.3
1946	18.2	18.1	18.3	18.4	18.5	18.7	19.8	20.2	20.4	20.8	21.3	21.5			19.5	18.1	8.3
1947	21.5	21.5	21.9	21.9	21.9	22.0	22.2	22.5	23.0	23.0	23.1	23.4			22.3	8.8	14.4
1948	23.7	23.5	23.4	23.8	23.9	24.1	24.4	24.5	24.5	24.4	24.2	24.1			24.1	3.0	8.1
1949	24.0	23.8	23.8	23.9	23.8	23.9	23.7	23.8	23.9	23.7	23.8	23.6			23.8	-2.1	-1.2
1950	23.5	23.5	23.6	23.6	23.7	23.8	24.1	24.3	24.4	24.6	24.7	25.0			24.1	5.9	1.3
1951	25.4	25.7	25.8	25.8	25.9	25.9	25.9	25.9	26.1	26.2	26.4	26.5			26.0	6.0	7.9
1952	26.5	26.3	26.3	26.4	26.4	26.5	26.7	26.7	26.7	26.7	26.7	26.7			26.5	.8	1.9
1953	26.6	26.5	26.6	26.6	26.7	26.8	26.8	26.9	26.9	27.0	26.9	26.9			26.7	.7	.8
1954	26.9	26.9	26.9	26.8	26.9	26.9	26.9	26.9	26.8	26.8	26.8	26.7			26.9	-.7	.7
1955	26.7	26.7	26.7	26.7	26.7	26.7	26.8	26.8	26.9	26.9	26.9	26.8			26.8	.4	-.4
1956	26.8	26.8	26.8	26.9	27.0	27.2	27.4	27.3	27.4	27.5	27.5	27.6			27.2	3.0	1.5
1957	27.6	27.7	27.8	27.9	28.0	28.1	28.3	28.3	28.3	28.3	28.4	28.4			28.1	2.9	3.3
1958	28.6	28.6	28.8	28.9	28.9	28.9	29.0	28.9	28.9	28.9	29.0	28.9			28.9	1.8	2.8
1959	29.0	28.9	28.9	29.0	29.0	29.1	29.2	29.2	29.3	29.4	29.4	29.4			29.1	1.7	.7
1960	29.3	29.4	29.4	29.5	29.5	29.6	29.6	29.6	29.6	29.8	29.8	29.8			29.6	1.4	1.7
1961	29.8	29.8	29.8	29.8	29.8	29.8	30.0	29.9	30.0	30.0	30.0	30.0			29.9	.7	1.0
1962	30.0	30.1	30.1	30.2	30.2	30.2	30.3	30.3	30.4	30.4	30.4	30.4			30.2	1.3	1.0
1963	30.4	30.4	30.5	30.5	30.5	30.6	30.7	30.7	30.7	30.8	30.8	30.9			30.6	1.6	1.3
1964	30.9	30.9	30.9	30.9	30.9	31.0	31.1	31.0	31.1	31.1	31.2	31.2			31.0	1.0	1.3
1965	31.2	31.2	31.3	31.4	31.4	31.6	31.6	31.6	31.6	31.7	31.7	31.8			31.5	1.9	1.6
1966	31.8	32.0	32.1	32.3	32.3	32.4	32.5	32.7	32.7	32.9	32.9	32.9			32.4	3.5	2.9
1967	32.9	32.9	33.0	33.1	33.2	33.3	33.4	33.5	33.6	33.7	33.8	33.9			33.4	3.0	3.1
1968	34.1	34.2	34.3	34.4	34.5	34.7	34.9	35.0	35.1	35.3	35.4	35.5			34.8	4.7	4.2
1969	35.6	35.8	36.1	36.3	36.4	36.6	36.8	37.0	37.1	37.3	37.5	37.7			36.7	6.2	5.5
1970	37.8	38.0	38.2	38.5	38.6	38.8	39.0	39.0	39.2	39.4	39.6	39.8			38.8	5.6	5.7
1971	39.8	39.9	40.0	40.1	40.3	40.6	40.7	40.8	40.8	40.9	40.9	41.1			40.5	3.3	4.4
1972	41.1	41.3	41.4	41.5	41.6	41.7	41.9	42.0	42.1	42.3	42.4	42.5			41.8	3.4	3.2
1973	42.6	42.9	43.3	43.6	43.9	44.2	44.3	45.1	45.2	45.6	45.9	46.2			44.4	8.7	6.2
1974	46.6	47.2	47.8	48.0	48.6	49.0	49.4	50.0	50.6	51.1	51.5	51.9			49.3	12.3	11.0
1975	52.1	52.5	52.7	52.9	53.2	53.6	54.2	54.3	54.6	54.9	55.3	55.5			53.8	6.9	9.1
1976	55.6	55.3	55.9	56.1	56.5	56.8	57.1	57.4	57.6	57.9	58.0	58.2			56.9	4.9	5.8
1977	58.5	59.1	59.5	60.0	60.3	60.7	61.0	61.2	61.4	61.6	61.9	62.1			60.6	6.7	6.5
1978	62.5	62.9	63.4	63.9	64.5	65.2	65.7	66.0	66.5	67.1	67.4	67.7			65.2	9.0	7.6
1979	68.3	69.1	69.8	70.6	71.5	72.3	73.1	73.8	74.6	75.2	75.9	76.7			72.6	13.3	11.3
1980	77.8	78.9	80.1	81.0	81.8	82.7	82.7	83.3	84.0	84.8	85.5	86.3			82.4	12.5	13.5
1981	87.0	37.9	88.5	89.1	89.8	90.6	91.6	92.3	93.2	93.4	93.7	94.0			90.9	8.9	10.3
1982	94.3	94.6	94.5	94.9	95.8	97.0	97.5	97.7	97.9	98.2	98.0	97.6			96.5	3.8	6.2
1983	97.8	97.9	97.9	98.6	99.2	99.5	99.9	100.2	100.7	101.0	101.2	101.3			99.6	3.3	3.2
1984	101.9	102.4	102.6	103.1	103.4	103.7	104.1	104.5	105.0	105.3	105.3	105.3	102.9	104.9	103.9	3.9	4.3

Year	Jan.	Feb.	Mar.	Apr.	May	June	July	Aug.	Sep.	Oct.	Nov.	Dec.	Semiannual Averages 1st Half	Semiannual Averages 2nd half	Annual Avg.	% Change From Previous Dec.	% Change From Previous Annual Avg.
1985	105.5	106.0	106.4	106.9	107.3	107.6	107.8	108.0	108.3	108.7	109.0	109.3	106.6	108.5	107.6	3.8	3.6
1986	109.6	109.3	108.8	108.6	108.9	109.5	109.5	109.7	110.2	110.3	110.4	110.5	109.1	110.1	109.6	1.1	1.9
1987	111.2	111.6	112.1	112.7	113.1	113.5	113.8	114.4	115.0	115.3	115.4	115.4	112.4	114.9	113.6	4.4	3.6
1988	115.7	116.0	116.5	117.1	117.5	118.0	118.5	119.0	119.3	120.2	120.3	120.5	116.8	119.7	118.3	4.4	4.1
1989	121.1	121.6	122.3	123.1	123.8	124.1	124.4	124.6	125.0	125.6	125.9	126.1	122.7	125.3	124.0	4.6	4.8
1990	127.4	128.0	128.7	128.9	129.2	129.9	130.4	131.6	132.7	133.5	133.8	133.8	128.7	132.6	130.7	6.1	5.4
1991	134.8	134.8	135.0	135.2	135.6	136.0	136.2	136.6	137.2	137.4	137.8	137.9	135.2	137.2	136.2	3.1	4.2
1992	138.1	138.6	139.3	139.5	139.7	140.2	140.5	140.9	141.3	141.8	142.0	141.9	139.2	141.4	140.3	2.9	3.0
1993	142.6	143.1	143.6	144.0	144.2	144.4	144.4	144.8	145.1	145.7	145.8	145.8	143.7	145.3	144.5	2.7	3.0
1994	146.2	146.7	147.2	147.4	147.5	148.0	148.4	149.0	149.4	149.5	149.7	149.7	147.2	149.3	148.2	2.7	2.6
1995	150.3	150.9	151.4	151.9	152.2	152.5	152.5	152.9	153.2	153.7	153.6	153.5	151.5	153.2	152.4	2.5	2.8
1996	154.4	154.9	155.7	156.3	156.6	156.7	157.0	157.3	157.8	158.3	158.6	158.6	155.8	157.9	156.9	3.3	3.0
1997	159.1	159.6	160.0	160.2	160.1	160.3	160.5	160.8	161.2	161.6	161.5	161.3	159.9	161.2	160.5	1.7	2.3
1998	161.6	161.9	162.2	-	-	-	-	-	-	-	-	-	-	-	-	-	-

Note: Index applies to a month as a whole, not to any specific date.
Source: United State Department of Labor. (1998). CPI Detailed Report, March, 1998. United State Department of Labor. Washington, D.C.

Appendix B

National Tourism Indicators

National Tourism Indicators, Part I

Supply of Tourism Commodities—Canada
Seasonally adjusted, millions of dollars and percentage change, preceding period

	Quarter								Year		
	95 I	95 II	95 III	95 IV	96 I	96 II	96 III	96 IV	1994	1995	1996
Transportation	**10,064**	**10,230**	**10,300**	**10,103**	**10,361**	**10,681**	**10,466**	**10,637**	**38,759**	**40,697**	**42,145**
	1.6	**1.6**	**0.7**	**-1.9**	**2.6**	**3.1**	**-2.0**	**1.6**	**5.6**	**5.0**	**3.6**
Passenger air	2,102	2,151	2,290	2,125	2,278	2,549	2,464	2,540	7,721	8,668	9,831
transport	4.0	2.36.5	-7.2	7.2	11.9	-3.3	3.1	8.4	12.3	13.4	
Passenger rail	45	48	49	44	46	48	48	45	187	186	187
transport	-2.2	6.7	2.1	-10.2	4.5	4.3	0.0	-6.3	6.9	-0.5	0.5
Interurban bus	125	131	135	127	123	124	124	113	492	518	484
transport	4.2	4.8	3.1	-5.9	-3.1	0.8	0.0	-8.9	0.4	5.3	-6.6
Vehicle rental	319	325	325	326	331	342	342	339	1,192	1,295	1,354
	5.6	1.9	0.0	0.3	1.5	3.3	0.0	-0.9	14.1	8.6	4.6
Vehicle repairs	2,774	2,763	2,808	2,767	2,731	2,703	2,653	2,591	10,745	11,112	10,678
and parts	0.1	-0.4	1.6	-1.5	-1.3	-1.0	-1.8	-2.3	7.8	3.4	-3.9
Vehicle fuel	3,536	3,646	3,523	3,535	3,648	3,698	3,610	3,798	13,826	14,240	14,754
	1.4	3.1	-3.4	0.3	3.2	1.4	-2.4	5.2	3.3	3.0	3.6
Other	1,163	1,166	1,170	1,179	1,204	1,217	1,225	1,211	4,596	4,678	4,857
transportation	0.6	0.3	0.3	0.8	2.1	1.1	0.7	- 1.1	1.6	1.8	3.8
Accommodation	**1,529**	**1,544**	**1,568**	**1,556**	**1,543**	**1,578**	**1,586**	**1,546**	**5,884**	**6,197**	**6,253**
	2.5	**1.0**	**1.6**	**-0.8**	**-0.8**	**2.3**	**0.5**	**-2.5**	**6.3**	**5.3**	**0.9**
Hotels	1,041	1,054	1,065	1,045	1,048	1,073	1,078	1,043	3,997	4,205	4,242
	4.8	1.2	1.0	-1.9	0.3	2.4	0.5	-3.2	6.5	5.2	0.9
Motels	243	247	246	250	240	247	247	241	947	986	975
	-1.2	1.6	-0.4	1.6	-4.0	2.9	0.0	-2.4	6.4	4.1	-1.1
Other	245	243	257	261	255	258	261	262	940	1,006	1,036
accomodation	-3.2	-0.8	5.8	1.6	-2.3	1.2	1.2	0.4	5.5	7.0	3.0

	Quarter								Year		
	95 I	95 II	95 III	95 IV	96 I	96 II	96 III	96 IV	1994	1995	1996
Food & beverage services	**7,479**	**7,788**	**8,052**	**8,186**	**8,261**	**8,402**	**8,546**	**8,728**	**29,395**	**31,505**	**33,937**
	-1.0	**4.1**	**3.4**	**1.7**	**0.9**	**1.7**	**1.7**	**2.1**	**5.9**	**7.2**	**7.7**
Meals, from accomodation services	471	482	488	483	489	502	497	489	1,829	1,924	1,977
	0.0	2.3	1.2	-1.0	1.2	2.7	-1.0	-1.6	6.4	5.2	2.8
Meals, from food & beverage services	5,039	5,274	5,474	5,625	5,668	5,796	5,935	6,119	19,740	21,412	23,518
	-0.8	4.7	3.8	2.8	0.8	2.3	2.4	3.1	5.9	8.5	9.8
Alcohol, from accomodation services	535	545	569	542	546	552	559	549	2,082	2,191	2,206
	0.0	1.9	4.4	-4.7	0.7	1.1	1.3	-1.8	6.6	5.2	0.7
Alcohol, from food & beverage services	1,150	1,173	1,209	1,230	1,250	1,241	1,234	1,244	4,601	4,762	4,969
	-2.9	2.0	3.1	1.7	1.6	-0.7	-0.6	0.8	5.1	3.5	4.3
Meals and alcohol, from other industries	284	314	312	306	308	311	321	327	1,143	1,216	1,267
	-0.4	10.6	-0.6	-1.9	0.7	1.0	3.2	1.9	6.0	6.4	4.2
Other tourism commodities	**3,085**	**3,388**	**3,376**	**3,327**	**3,370**	**3,417**	**3,527**	**3,586**	**12,203**	**13,176**	**13,900**
	-1.0	**9.8**	**-0.4**	**-1.5**	**1.3**	**1.4**	**3.2**	**1.7**	**16.0**	**8.0**	**5.5**
Recreation and entertainment	2,904	3,204	3,189	3,145	3,181	3,215	3,326	3,385	11,494	12,442	13,107
	-1.1	10.3	-0.5	-1.4	1.1	1.1	3.5	1.8	16.8	8.2	5.3
Travel agency services	148	151	156	148	156	166	163	165	584	603	650
	-1.3	2.0	3.3	-5.1	5	.4	6.4	-1.8	1.2	3.5	3.3
Convention fees	33	33	31	34	33	36	38	36	125	131	143
	6.5	0.0	-6.1	9.7	-2.9	9.1	5.6	-5.3	10.6	4.8	9.2
Total tourism commodities	**22,157**	**22,950**	**23,296**	**23,172**	**23,535**	**24,078**	**24,125**	**24,497**	**86,241**	**91,575**	**96,235**
	0.4	**3.6**	**1.5**	**-0.5**	**1.6**	**2.3**	**0.2**	**1.5**	**7.1**	**6.2**	**5.1**

Source:Statistics Canada, 1996. National Tourism Indicators, Fourth Quarter, 1996. Catalogue no. 13-009-XPB. Ottawa, Ontario.

National Tourism Indicators, Part II

Tourism Demand—Canada
Seasonally adjusted, millions of dollars and percentage change, preceding period

	Quarter								Year		
	95 I	95 II	95 III	95 IV	96 I	96 II	96 III	96 IV	1994	1995	1996
Transportation	**4,275**	**4,280**	**4,451**	**4,382**	**4,485**	**4,776**	**4,692**	**4,764**	**16,181**	**17,388**	**18,717**
	1.2	**0.1**	**4.0**	**-1.6**	**2.4**	**6.5**	**-1.8**	**1.5**	**6.6**	**7.5**	**7.6**
Passenger air	1,937	1,974	2,075	1,994	2,112	2,368	2,298	2,371	7,108	7,980	9,149
transport	3.0	1.9	5.1	-3.9	5.9	12.1	-3.0	3.2	8.4	12.3	14.6
Passenger rail	38	40	40	38	39	42	41	39	156	156	161
transport	-5.0	5.3	0.0	-5.0	2.6	7.7	-2.4	-4.9	6.8	0.0	3.2
Interurban bus	113	114	116	114	110	112	114	102	435	457	438
transport	2.7	0.9	1.8	-1.7	-3.5	1.8	1.8	-10.5	0.7	5.1	-4.2
Vehicle rental	264	268	270	273	278	285	285	278	989	1,075	1,126
	4.8	1.5	0.7	1.1	1.8	2.5	0.0	-2.5	14.1	8.7	4.7
Vehicle repairs	524	518	536	536	522	516	513	509	2,044	2,114	2,060
and parts	-1.3	-1.1	3.5	0.0	-2.6	-1.1	-0.6	-0.8	7.8	3.4	-2.6
Vehicle fuel	1,148	1,119	1,167	1,172	1,172	1,192	1,182	1,204	4,473	4,606	4,750
	-1.6	-2.5	4.3	0.4	0.0	1.7	-0.8	1.9	3.3	3.0	3.1
Other	251	247	247	255	252	261	259	261	976	1,000	1,033
transportation	2.4	-1.6	0.0	3.2	-1.2	3.6	-0.8	0.8	3.4	2.5	3.3
Accommodation	**1,368**	**1,379**	**1,403**	**1,389**	**1,379**	**1,410**	**1,404**	**1,380**	**5,263**	**5,539**	**5,573**
	2.9	**0.8**	**1.7**	**-1.0**	**-0.7**	**2.2**	**-0.4**	**-1.7**	**6.4**	**5.2**	**0.6**
Hotels	954	967	972	950	962	986	982	955	3,652	3,843	3,885
	5.8	1.4	0.5	-2.3	1.3	2.5	-0.4	-2.7	6.5	5.2	1.1
Motels	231	235	236	239	227	233	231	230	904	941	921
	1.3	1.7	0.4	1.3	-5.0	2.6	-0.9	-0.4	6.5	4.1	-2.1
Other	183	177	195	200	190	191	191	195	707	755	767
accommodation	-5.2	-3.3	10.2	2.6	-5.0	0.5	0.0	2.1	5.5	6.8	1.6
Food & beverage	**1,960**	**1,969**	**1,969**	**2,046**	**2,071**	**2,118**	**2,104**	**2,145**	**7,399**	**7,944**	**8,438**
services	**0.6**	**0.5**	**0.0**	**3.9**	**1.2**	**2.3**	**-0.7**	**1.9**	**5.9**	**7.4**	**6.2**
Meals, from											
accomodation	246	248	250	253	251	260	256	255	947	997	1,022
services	0.4	0.8	0.8	1.2	-0.8	3.6	-1.5	-0.4	6.4	5.3	2.5
Meals, from											
food & beverage	1,368	1,376	1,375	1,435	1,463	1,492	1,488	1,524	5,120	5,554	5,967
services	0.8	0.6	-0.1	4.4	2.0	2.0	-0.3	2.4	5.9	8.5	7.4
Alcohol, from											
accomodation	88	88	89	91	89	93	92	92	338	356	366
services	1.1	0.0	1.1	2.2	-2.2	4.5	-1.1	0.0	6.6	5.3	2.8
Alcohol, from											
food & beverage	174	174	172	180	181	183	182	185	676	700	731
services	-1.7	0.0	-1.1	4.7	0.6	1.1	-0.5	1.6	5.0	3.6	4.4
Meals and alcohol,											
from other	84	83	83	87	87	90	86	89	318	337	352
industries	1.2	-1.2	0.0	4.8	0.0	3.4	-4.4	3.5	6.0	6.0	4.5
Other tourism	**1,022**	**1,036**	**1,049**	**1,053**	**1,063**	**1,096**	**1,097**	**1,116**	**3,874**	**4,160**	**4,372**
commodities	**0.6**	**1.4**	**1.3**	**0.4**	**0.9**	**3.1**	**0.1**	**1.7**	**14.4**	**7.4**	**5.1**
Recreation and	847	857	869	876	878	900	901	921	3,188	3,449	3,600
entertainment	0.8	1.2	1.4	0.8	0.2	2.5	0.1	2.2	16.8	8.2	4.4
Travel agency	145	148	152	146	153	162	160	162	572	591	637
services	-2.0	2.1	2.7	-3.9	4.8	5.9	-1.2	1.3	3.6	3.3	7.8
Convention fees	30	31	28	31	32	34	36	33	114	120	135
	7.1	3.3	-9.7	10.7	3.2	6.3	5.9	-8.3	10.7	5.3	12.5
Total tourism	**8,625**	**8,664**	**8,872**	**8,870**	**8,998**	**9,400**	**9,297**	**9,405**	**32,717**	**35,031**	**37,100**
commodities	**1.2**	**0.5**	**2.4**	**-0.0**	**1.4**	**4.5**	**-1.1**	**1.2**	**7.3**	**7.1**	**5.9**

Source: Statistics Canada, 1996. National Tourism Indicators, Fourth Quarter, 1996. Catalogue no. 13-009-XPB. Ottawa, Ontario.

National Tourism Indicators, Part III

Tourism Domestic Demand—Canada
Seasonally adjusted, millions of dollars and percentage change, preceding period

	Quarter								Year		
	95 I	95 II	95 III	95 IV	96 I	96 II	96 III	96 IV	1994	1995	1996
Transportation	**3,291**	**3,272**	**3,417**	**3,306**	**3,391**	**3,607**	**3,556**	**3,600**	**12,639**	**13,286**	**14,154**
	0.7	**-0.6**	**4.4**	**-3.2**	**2.6**	**6.4**	**-1.4**	**1.2**	**4.1**	**5.1**	**6.5**
Passenger air	1,470	1,488	1,561	1,456	1,582	1,786	1,716	1,771	5,409	5,975	6,855
transport	3.0	1.2	4.9	-6.7	8.7	12.9	-3.9	3.2	6.1	10.5	14.7
Passenger rail	18	18	17	16	15	16	16	16	81	69	63
transport	0.0	0.0	-5.6	-5.9	-6.3	6.7	0.0	0.0	-4.7	-14.8	-8.7
Interurban bus	56	57	55	52	49	47	46	40	232	220	182
transport	5.7	1.8	-3.5	-5.5	-5.8	-4.1	-2.1	-13.0	-8.3	-5.2	-17.3
Vehicle rental	164	165	163	163	164	165	165	164	637	655	658
	2.5	0.6	-1.2	0.0	0.6	0.6	0.0	-0.6	10.8	2.8	0.5
Vehicle repairs	489	483	502	501	485	479	480	473	1,916	1,975	1,917
and parts	-1.4	-1.2	3.9	-0.2	-3.2	-1.2	0.2	-1.5	7.3	3.1	-2.9
Vehicle fuel	940	912	972	971	951	964	984	987	3,741	3,795	3,886
	-2.4	-3.0	6.6	-0.1	-2.1	1.4	2.1	0.3	1.1	1.4	2.4
Other transportation	154	149	147	147	145	150	149	149	623	597	593
	2.0	-3.2	-1.3	0.0	-1.4	3.4	-0.7	0.0	-2.5	-4.2	-0.7
Accommodation	**991**	**990**	**999**	**984**	**971**	**967**	**954**	**953**	**3,936**	**3,964**	**3,845**
	0.8	**-0.1**	**0.9**	**-1.5**	**-1.3**	**-0.4**	**-1.3**	**-0.1**	**4.0**	**0.7**	**-3.0**
Hotels	671	676	671	648	655	653	638	633	2,655	2,666	2,579
	4.5	0.7	-0.7	-3.4	1.1	-0.3	-2.3	-0.8	3.8	0.4	-3.3
Motels	180	183	181	184	175	174	173	173	727	728	695
	-4.3	1.7	-1.1	1.7	-4.9	-0.6	-0.6	0.0	5.1	0.1	-4.5
Other	140	131	147	152	141	140	143	147	554	570	571
accomodation	-8.5	-6.4	12.2	3.4	-7.2	-0.7	2.1	2.8	3.6	2.9	0.2
Food & beverage	**1,316**	**1,325**	**1,323**	**1,367**	**1,370**	**1,395**	**1,414**	**1,435**	**5,064**	**5,331**	**5,614**
services	**-0.8**	**0.7**	**-0.2**	**3.3**	**0.2**	**1.8**	**1.4**	**1.5**	**2.3**	**5.3**	**5.3**
Meals, from											
accommodation	140	142	144	142	136	139	140	138	565	568	553
services	-2.1	1.4	1.4	-1.4	-4.2	2.2	0.7	-1.4	1.4	0.5	-2.6
Meals, from											
food & beverage	944	952	949	988	1,000	1,017	1,035	1,056	3,585	3,833	4,108
services	-0.3	0.8	-0.3	4.1	1.2	1.7	1.8	2.0	2.5	6.9	7.2
Alcohol, from											
accomodation	55	55	56	56	54	56	56	56	217	222	222
services	0.0	0.0	1.8	0.0	-3.6	3.7	0.0	0.0	2.8	2.3	0.0
Alcohol, from											
food & beverage	120	120	118	123	121	122	124	126	478	481	493
services	-3.2	0.0	-1.7	4.2	-1.6	0.8	1.6	1.6	1.7	0.6	2.5
Meals and alcohol,											
from other	57	56	56	58	59	61	59	59	219	227	238
industries	0.0	-1.8	0.0	3.6	1.7	3.4	-3.3	0.0	2.3	3.7	4.8
Other tourism	**780**	**792**	**804**	**798**	**800**	**828**	**841**	**854**	**2,990**	**3,174**	**3,323**
commodities	**0.0**	**1.5**	**1.5**	**-0.7**	**0.3**	**3.5**	**1.6**	**1.5**	**14.5**	**6.2**	**4.7**
Recreation and	613	622	632	631	625	642	656	669	2,335	2,498	2,592
entertainment	0.2	1.5	1.6	-0.2	-1.0	2.7	2.2	2.0	17.7	7.0	3.8
Travel agency	141	144	148	141	148	157	155	157	558	574	617
services	-2.1	2.1	2.8	-4.7	5.0	6.1	-1.3	1.3	3.3	2.9	7.5
Convention fees	26	26	24	26	27	29	30	28	97	102	114
	8.3	0.0	-7.7	8.3	3.8	7.4	3.4	-6.7	11.5	5.2	11.8
Total tourism	**6,378**	**6,379**	**6,543**	**6,455**	**6,532**	**6,797**	**6,765**	**6,842**	**24,629**	**25,755**	**26,936**
commodities	**0.3**	**0.0**	**2.6**	**-1.3**	**1.2**	**4.1**	**-0.5**	**1.1**	**4.9**	**4.6**	**4.6**

Source: Statistics Canada, 1996. National Tourism Indicators, Fourth Quarter, 1996. Catalogue no. 13-009-XPB. Ottawa, Ontario.

National Tourism Indicators, Part IV

Tourism Exports—Canada
Seasonally adjusted, millions of dollars and percentage change, preceding period

	Quarter								Year		
	95 I	95 II	95 III	95 IV	96 I	96 II	96 III	96 IV	1994	1995	1996
Transportation	**984**	**1,008**	**1,034**	**1,076**	**1,094**	**1,169**	**1,136**	**1,164**	**3,542**	**4,102**	**4,563**
	2.7	**2.4**	**2.6**	**4.1**	**1.7**	**6.9**	**-2.8**	**2.5**	**16.7**	**15.8**	**11.2**
Passenger air	467	486	514	538	530	582	582	600	1,699	2,005	2,294
transport	2.9	4.1	5.8	4.7	-1.5	9.8	0.0	3.1	16.4	18.0	14.4
Passenger rail	20	22	23	22	24	26	25	23	75	87	98
transport	-9.1	10.0	4.5	-4.3	9.1	8.3	-3.8	-8.0	23.0	16.0	12.6
Interurban bus	57	57	61	62	61	65	68	62	203	237	256
transport	0.0	0.0	7.0	1.6	-1.6	6.6	4.6	-8.8	13.4	16.7	8.0
Vehicle rental	100	103	107	110	114	120	120	114	352	420	468
	8.7	3.0	3.9	2.8	3.6	5.3	0.0	-5.0	20.5	19.3	11.4
Vehicle repairs	35	35	34	35	37	37	33	36	128	139	143
and parts	0.0	0.0	-2.9	2.9	5.7	0.0	-10.8	9.1	16.4	8.6	2.9
Vehicle fuel	208	207	195	201	221	228	198	217	732	811	864
	2.0	-0.5	-5.8	3.1	10.0	3.2	-13.2	9.6	16.6	10.8	6.5
Other transportation	97	98	100	108	107	111	110	112	353	403	440
	3.2	1.0	2.0	8.0	-0.9	3.7	-0.9	1.8	15.7	14.2	9.2
Accommodation	**377**	**389**	**404**	**405**	**408**	**443**	**450**	**427**	**1,327**	**1,575**	**1,728**
	9.0	**3.2**	**3.9**	**0.2**	**0.7**	**8.6**	**1.6**	**-5.1**	**14.1**	**18.7**	**9.7**
Hotels	283	291	301	302	307	333	344	322	997	1,177	1,306
	8.8	2.8	3.4	0.3	1.7	8.5	3.3	-6.4	14.5	18.1	11.0
Motels	51	52	55	55	52	59	58	57	177	213	226
	10.9	2.0	5.8	0.0	-5.5	13.5	-1.7	-1.7	12.7	20.3	6.1
Other	43	46	48	48	49	51	48	48	153	185	196
accommodation	7.5	7.0	4.3	0.0	2.1	4.1	-5.9	0.0	13.3	20.9	5.9
Food & beverage	**644**	**644**	**646**	**679**	**701**	**723**	**690**	**710**	**2,335**	**2,613**	**2,824**
services	**3.4**	**0.0**	**0.3**	**5.1**	**3.2**	**3.1**	**4.6**	**2.9**	**14.6**	**11.9**	**8.1**
Meals, from											
accommodation	106	106	106	111	115	121	116	117	382	429	469
services	3.9	0.0	0.0	4.7	3.6	5.2	-4.1	0.9	14.7	12.3	9.3
Meals, from											
food & beverage	424	424	426	447	463	475	453	468	1,535	1,721	1,859
services	3.4	0.0	0.5	4.9	3.6	2.6	-4.6	3.3	14.7	12.1	8.0
Alcohol, from											
accommodation	33	33	33	35	35	37	36	36	121	134	144
services	3.1	0.0	0.0	0.1	0.0	5.7	-2.7	0.0	14.2	10.7	7.5
Alcohol, from											
food & beverage	54	54	54	57	60	61	58	59	198	219	238
services	1.9	0.0	0.0	5.6	5.3	1.7	-4.9	1.7	13.8	10.6	8.7
Meals and alcohol,											
from other	27	27	27	29	28	29	27	30	99	110	114
industries	3.8	0.0	0.0	7.4	-3.4	3.6	-6.9	11.1	15.1	11.1	3.6
Other tourism	**242**	**244**	**245**	**255**	**263**	**268**	**256**	**262**	**884**	**986**	**1,049**
commodities	**2.5**	**0.8**	**0.4**	**4.1**	**3.1**	**1.9**	**-4.5**	**2.3**	**14.2**	**11.5**	**6.4**
Recreation and	234	235	237	245	253	258	245	252	853	951	1,008
entertainment	2.6	0.4	0.9	3.4	3.3	2.0	-5.0	2.9	14.3	11.5	6.0
Travel agency	4	4	4	5	5	5	5	5	14	17	20
services	0.0	0.0	0.0	25.0	0.0	0.0	0.0	0.0	16.7	21.4	17.6
Convention fees	4	5	4	5	5	5	6	5	17	18	21
	0.0	25.0	-20.0	25.0	0.0	0.0	20.0	-16.7	6.3	5.9	16.7
Total tourism	**2,247**	**2,285**	**2,329**	**2,415**	**2,466**	**2,603**	**2,532**	**2,563**	**8,088**	**9,276**	**10,164**
commodities	**3.9**	**1.7**	**1.9**	**3.7**	**2.1**	**5.6**	**-2.7**	**1.2**	**15.4**	**14.7**	**9.6**

Source: Statistics Canada, 1996. National Tourism Indicators, Fourth Quarter, 1996. Catalogue no. 13-009-XPB. Ottawa, Ontario.

National Tourism Indicators, Part V

Employment Generated by Tourism
Seasonally adjusted, thousands of employed persons and percentage change, preceding period

	Quarter								Year		
	95 I	95 II	95 III	95 IV	96 I	96 II	96 III	96 IV	1994	1995	1996
Total tourism	**368.8**	**377.5**	**382.2**	**384.1**	**391.8**	**388.5**	**380.9**	**384.1**	**371.9**	**378.2**	**386.3**
industries	**-1.3**	**2.4**	**1.2**	**0.5**	**2.0**	**-0.8**	**-2.0**	**0.8**	**2.8**	**1.7**	**2.2**
Transportation	**79.1**	**81.2**	**79.4**	**81.5**	**82.6**	**83.7**	**81.3**	**85.0**	**80.2**	**80.3**	**83.2**
	-1.6	**2.7**	**-2.2**	**2.6**	**1.3**	**1.3**	**-2.9**	**4.6**	**1.2**	**0.2**	**3.5**
Air transportation	36.2	36.2	35.4	37.0	38.6	38.0	37.8	40.3	35.8	36.2	38.7
	-2.4	0.0	-2.2	4.5	4.3	-1.6	-0.5	6.6	3.7	1.2	6.8
Railway	5.0	5.0	5.0	4.9	4.6	4.5	4.3	4.2	5.2	5.0	4.4
transportation	-2.0	0.0	0.0	-2.0	-6.1	-2.2	-4.4	-2.3	-3.3	-3.4	-11.6
Water	2.4	2.3	2.4	2.5	2.4	2.3	2.2	2.3	2.5	2.4	2.3
transportation	-4.0	-4.2	4.3	4.2	-4.0	-4.2	-4.3	4.5	-1.0	-2.0	-4.2
Bus transportation	11.9	12.4	12.4	13.2	13.3	13.3	12.5	13.1	12.3	12.5	13.1
	-0.8	4.2	0.0	6.5	0.8	0.0	-6.0	4.8	1.4	1.6	4.6
Taxicabs	11.2	11.5	11.4	12.0	12.0	11.7	10.9	11.3	12.4	11.5	11.5
	-3.4	2.7	-0.9	5.3	0.0	-2.5	-6.8	3.7	-7.5	-7.1	-0.4
Vehicle rental	2.4	13.8	12.8	11.9	11.7	13.9	13.6	13.8	12.1	12.7	13.3
& leasing	2.5	11.3	-7.2	-7.0	-1.7	18.8	-2.2	1.5	6.1	4.9	4.1
Accommodation	**126.5**	**129.3**	**134.1**	**134.6**	**140.8**	**137.2**	**135.0**	**134.0**	**130.2**	**131.1**	**136.8**
	-2.8	**2.2**	**3.7**	**0.4**	**4.6**	**-2.6**	**-1.6**	**-0.7**	**5.1**	**0.7**	**4.3**
Food & beverage	**133.5**	**135.7**	**137.5**	**136.6**	**137.9**	**137.6**	**134.9**	**136.2**	**130.6**	**135.8**	**136.7**
services	**0.5**	**1.6**	**1.3**	**-0.7**	**1.0**	**-0.2**	**-2.0**	**1.0**	**0.6**	**4.0**	**0.6**
Other tourism	**29.7**	**31.3**	**31.2**	**31.4**	**30.5**	**30.0**	**29.7**	**28.9**	**31.0**	**30.9**	**29.8**
industries	**-2.3**	**5.4**	**-0.3**	**0.6**	**-2.9**	**-1.6**	**-1.0**	**-2.7**	**6.6**	**-0.4**	**-3.6**
Recreation and	20.9	23.1	23.1	23.0	22.1	21.4	20.8	20.2	22.9	22.5	21.1
entertainment	-5.9	10.5	0.0	-0.4	-3.9	-3.2	-2.8	-2.9	5.9	-1.6	-6.2
Travel agencies	8.8	8.2	8.1	8.4	8.4	8.6	8.9	8.7	8.1	8.4	8.7
	7.3	-6.8	-1.2	3.7	0.0	2.4	3.5	-2.2	8.7	3.1	3.3
Total employment,	**9,510**	**9,525**	**9,524**	**9,531**	**9,542**	**9,539**	**9,539**	**9,517**	**9,524**	**9,522**	**9,534**
business sector	**-1.0**	**0.2**	**-0.0**	**0.1**	**0.1**	**-0.0**	**0.0**	**-0.2**	**4.1**	**-0.0**	**0.1**

Source: Statistics Canada, 1996. National Tourism Indicators, Fourth Quarter, 1996. Catalogue no. 13-009-XPB. Ottawa, Ontario.

Appendix C

The Weighting Method of Tourism Attractiveness Index

The Churchman-Ackoff-Arnoff Method for Weighting Objectives

This method involves the systematic comparison of various "outcomes" (O_m) (in the context of assessing regional tourism attractiveness, the "outcomes" are the various regional characteristics) in order to assign weights proportional to the importance or desirability of each outcome. The general symbolic formulation of the method of estimating weights (vj) associated with the various outcomes or regional characteristics is quite formidable in appearance but not in practice.

1. Rank the outcomes in their order of value. Let O_1 represent the most valued, O_2, the next most valued, . . . and O_m the least valued.
2. Assign the value 1.00 to O_1 (i.e., $v_j = 1.00$) and assign values that appear suitable to each of the other outcomes.
3. Compare O_1 versus $O_2 + \ldots + O_m$

   3.1 If O_1 is preferable to $O_2 + O_3 + \ldots + O_m$, adjust (if necessary) the value of v_1 so that $v_1 > v_2 + v_3 + \ldots + v_m$. In this adjustment, as in all others, attempt to keep the relative values of the adjusted group (v_2, v_3, etc.) invariant. Proceed to step 4.

   3.2 If O_1 and $O_2 + O_3 + \ldots + O_m$ are equally referred, adjust (if necessary) the value of v_1 so that $v_1 = v_2 + v_3 + \ldots + v_m$. Proceed to step 4.

3.3 If O_1 is preferred less than $O_2 + O_3 + \ldots + O_m$, adjust (if necessary) the value of v_1 so that $v_1 < v_2 + v_3 + \ldots + v_m$.

3.3.1 Compare O_1 versus $O_2 + O_3 + \ldots + O_{m-1}$.

3.3.1.1 If O_1 is preferred, adjust (if necessary) the values so that $v_1 > v_2 + v_3 + \ldots + v_{m-1}$. Proceed to step 4.

3.3.1.2 If O_1 and $O_2 + O_3 + \ldots + O_{m-1}$ are equally referred, adjust (if necessary) the values so that $v_1 = v_2 + v_3 + \ldots + v_{m-1}$. Proceed to step 4.

3.3.1.3 If O_1 is preferred less than $O_2 + O_3 + \ldots + O_{m-1}$, adjust (if necessary) the values so that $v_1 = v_2 + v_3 + \ldots + v_{m-1}$.

3.3.1.3.1 Compare O_1 versus $O_2 + O_3 + \ldots + O_{m-2}$, etc. until either O_1 is preferred or is equal to the rest, then proceed to step 4, or until O_1 is compared to just $O_2 + O_3$. Then proceed to step 4.

4. Compare O_2 versus $O_3 + O_4 + \ldots + O_m$ and proceed as in step 3.
5. Continue until the comparison of O_{m-2} versus $O_{m-1} + O_m$ is completed.
6. Convert each v_j into a normalized v_j', dividing v_j by $S\Sigma vj$. Then $S\Sigma v_j$ will be equal to 1.00.

It should be noted that the resulting estimated values are relative; that is, deletion or addition of an outcome (or regional characteristic) will affect the values obtained for all other outcomes. Furthermore, the estimated values obtained for a set of outcomes may chance over time if the true values chance.

Note : The + sign here designates the logical connective 'and'.

Sources: Churchman, C. N., Ackoff, R.I., and Arnoff, E. L. (1957). *Introduction to Operation Research.* New York: Wiley. Chapter 6.
Smith, S. L. J. (1995). *Tourism Analysis: a handbook.* New York: Longman, Harlow.

References

Antoniou, A. (1995). "Futures Trading, Information and Spot Price Volatility: Evidence for the FTSE-100 Stock Index Futures Contract Using GARCH." *Journal of Banking and Finance.* 19 (Apr.): 117–129.

Auger, J. (1974). *Analyse Factorielle et Evaluation d'Attraction de Sites Recreatifs.* Quebec: Government du Quebec. (Ministere du Tourisme, de la Chasse et de lay Peche, Service de la Recherche, January 1974, Rapport Technique No. 2).

Backman, K.F. and Uysal, M. (1987). "Development of a Tourism Index for Texas." In *Travel and Tourism: Thrive or Survive?* (Travel and Tourism Research Association, Eighteenth Annual Conference, Seattle, Washington). pp. 211–217.

Backman, K.F., Uysal, M., and Backman, S.J. (1992). "Index Number: A Tourism Managerial and Policy-Making Tool." *Journal of Applied Recreation Research.* 17 (2): 158–177.

Beaman, J. (1974). "Three Methods for Measuring the Attractiveness of a Park—A Comparison," (Parks Canada, Ottawa: CORD Technical Note No. 9, May 1974), (mimeo).

Bond, M.E., and B. McDonald. (1978). "Tourism Barometers: The Arizona Case." *Journal of Travel Research.* 17 (Fall): 14–17.

Bonn, M.A. and Brand, R.R. (1995). "Identifying Market Potential: The Application of Brand Development Indexing to Pleasure Travel." *Journal of Travel Research.* (Fall): 31–35.

Bowley, A.L. (1902). *Elements of Statistics.* Snd ed. London. p. 217.

Boyer, M. (1972). *Le Tourisme.* Paris: Editions du Seuil.

Cesario, F.J. (1973). "Final Report on Estimating Park Attractiveness, Population Center Emissiveness and the Effect of Distance (Location) in Outdoor Recreation Travel." Ottawa: Department of Indiana and Northern Affairs. (CORD Technical Note, No. 4, 1973). (mimeo).

Cesario, F.J., Goldstone, S.E., and Knetsch, J.L. (1969). *A Report on Outdoor Recreation Demands and Values to Middle Atlantic Utility Group.* Columbus: Batelle Memorial Institute. p. 38.

Cesario, F.J. and Knetsch, J.L. (1969). "A Recreation Site Demand and Benefit Estimation." p. 2. (mimeo).

Chan, K. and Chung, Y.P. (1995). "Vector Autoregression or Simultaneous Equations Model? The Intraday Relationship Between Index Arbitrage and Market Volatility." *Journal of Banking and Finance.* 19 (Apr.): 173–9.

Cheung, H.K. (1972). "A Day-Use Park Visitation Model," *Journal of Leisure Research.* 4(Spring): 139–142.

Chaudhry, R., Rogers, M. and Kosinski, M. (1994). "The Best Places in America to Open a Restaurant." *Restaurant & Institutions.* 104/13: 34–39.

Cherny, S.S., Fulker, D.W., and Emde, R.N. (1994). "A Developmental-Genetic Analysis of Continuity and Change in the Bayley Mental Development Index from 14 to 24 Months." *Psychological Science.* 5: 354–60.

Churchman, C.N., Ackoff, R.I., and Arnoff, E.L. (1957). *Introduction to Operation Research.* New York: Wiley. Chapter 6.

Clary, D. (1977). "La facada littoral de Paris: Le tourisme sur sa cote Normande". *Etude Geographique.* Paris: Editions Ophyrys.

Clawson, M. and Knetsch, J.L. (1963). "Outdoor Recreation Research: Some Concepts and Suggested Areas of Study." *Natural Resources Journal.* 3: 2.

Clayton-Matthews, A., Kodrzycki, Y.K., and Swaine, D. (1994). "Indexes of Economic Indicators: What Can They Tell Us about the New England Economy?" *New England Economic Review.* (Nov./Dec.) p. 17–41.

Clough, P.W.J. (1987). "A Note on the Use of the Trip Index in Travel Cost Analysis." *Journal of Travel Research.* (Summer): 29–31.

Coffey, W.J. (1981). *Geography: Towards a General Spatial Systems Approach.* London: Methuen and Company. pp. 101–104.

Coopers & Lybrand Consulting (1996). Canadian Tourism Commission: Domestic Tourism Market Research Study—Main Report. (March 1996.)

Crawford, A. (1993). *Measurement Biases in the Canadian CPI.* Bank of Canada. (Technical Report No. 64.)

Defert, P. (1967). "Le taux de fonction: Mise au point et critique." Aix-en Province, France: Les cabiers du tourisme. Centre des Hautes Etudes Touristiques. C-13.

Diamond, J. (1977). "Tourism's Role in Economic Development: The Case Reexamined," *Economic Development and Cultural Change.* 25(April): 539–553.

Dilts, David A. (1994). "The Consumer Price Index as a Standard in Negotiations and Arbitration." *Journal of Collective Negotiations in the Public Sector.* 23(4): 279–286.

Ellis, J.B. (1963). *Analysis of Socioeconomic Systems by Physical Systems Techniques,* Unpublished Ph.D. dissertation. East Lansing: Michigan State University.

Fesenmaier, D.R. and Lieber, S.R. (1988). "Destination Diversification as an Indicator of Activity Compatibility: An Exploratory Analysis." *Leisure Science.* 10:167-178.

Forsyth, P., and Dwyer, L. (1996). *Australian Tourism: Is It Price Competitive?* Canberra, Australia: Commonweath Department of Industry, Science and Tourism, University of Western Sydney Macarthur.

Fridgen, J.D. (1987). "Use of Cognitive Maps to Determine Perceived Tourism Regions." *Leisure Sciences.* 9: 101–117.

Fridgen, J.D. Udd, E. and Deale, C. (1983). "Cognitive Maps of Tourism Regions in Michigan." In *Proceedings of the Applied Geography Conference*. Toronto, Canada: Ryerson Polytechnic Institute. pp. 262–272.

Frisoni, G.B., Franzoni, S., and Rozzini, R. (1994). "A Nutritional Index Predicting Mortality in the Nursing Home." *Journal of the American Geriatrics Society.* 42: 1167–72.

Gardavsky, V. (1977). "Second Homes in Czechoslovakia." In Coppock J.T. (ed.), *Second Homes: Curse or Blessing?* London: Pergamon. pp. 83–94.

Gearing, C.E., Swart, W.W., and Var, T.C. (1974). "Establishing a Measure of Tourist Attractiveness." *Journal of Travel Research.* 12: 1–8.

Georges, C. (1995). "Economic Gains Fail to Increase Benefits, Wages." *Wall Street Journal.* (Eastern Edition) (Feb. 1) p. A2+.

Gray, H. P. (1966). "The Demand for International Travel by the United States and Canada," *International Economic Review.* 7(January): 83-92.

Gray, H. P. (1970). *International Travel—International Trade.* Lexington: Heath Lexington Books.

Gu, Z. (1994). "Hospitality Investment Return, Risk, and Performance Indexes: A Ten-Year Examination." *Hospitality Research Journal.* 17 (3): 17–26.

Hatcher, S.L., Nadeau, M.S., and Walsh, L.K. (1994). "The Teaching of Empty for High School and College Students: Testing Rogerian Methods with the Interpersonal Reactivity Index." *Adolescence.* 29 (Winter): 961–74.

Hinch, T.D. (1990). "A Spatial Analysis of Tourist Accommodation in Ontario: 1974–1978." *Journal of Applied Recreation Research.* 15(4): 239–264.

Hogan, T.D., and Rex, T.R. (1984). "Monitoring Current Activity in Arizona with a Quarterly Tourism Model." *Journal of Travel Research.* 23: 22–26.

Huan, T.C. (1997). *Monitoring and Exploring U.S. International Travellers' Behaviors in Canada: Development and Application of Index Scores.* West Lafayette, IN: Dept. of Forestry and Natural Resources, Purdue University.

Hudman, L.E. (1979). "Origin Regions of International Tourism." *Weiner Geographische Schriftew.* 53/54: 43–49.

Hudman, L.E. (1980). *Tourist: A Shrinking World.* Columbus: GRID.

Jalali-Farahani, H.R., Slack, D.C., and Kopec, D.M. (1994). "Evaluation of Resistances for Bermudagrass Turf Crop Water Stress Index Models." *Agronomy Journal.* 86: 574–81.

Joseph, H., and Judd, G.D. (1974). "Estimates of Tourism Demand: Latin American." In Krause, W., Judd, G.D., and Joseph, H. (eds.), *International Tourism and Latin American Development*. Austin: University of Texas Press. pp. 25–42.

Judd, G.D., and Rulison, M.V.E. (1983). "An Index of North Carolina Travel and Tourism." *Journal of Travel Research.* 21 (Winter): 13–15.

Keogh, B. (1984). "The Measurement of Spatial Variations in Tourist Activity." *Annals of Tourism Research.* 11: 267–282.

Kwack, Y.S. (1972). "Effects of Income and Prices on Travel Spending Abroad, 1960 III–1976 IV," *International Economic Review.* 13(June): 245–256.

Lee, Y. (1979). A Nearest Neighbor Spatial Association Measure for the Analysis of Firm Interdependence. *Environment and Planning A.* 11: 169–76.

Leiper, N. (1989). "Main Destination Ratio: Analyses of Tourist Flows." *Annals of Tourism Research.* 16: 530–541.

Little, J. S. (1980). "International Travel in the U.S. Balance of Payments," *New England Economic Review.* (May–June): 42–55.

Loeb, D.P. (1982). "International Travel to the United States: An Economic Evaluation," *Annuals of Tourism Research.* 9(1): 7–20.

Love, E.B., Nowicki, S., Jr., and Duke, M.P. (1994). "The Emory Dyssemia Index: A Brief Screening Instrument for the Identification of Nonverbal Language Deficits in Elementary School Children." *The Journal of Psychology.* 128: 703–5.

Mendenhall, W. and Reinmuth, J. (1982). *Statistics of Management and Economics.* Bistow: Daxbury Press.

Merriam-Webster, Inc. (1983). *Webster's Ninth New Collegiate Dictionary.* Springfield, Massachusetts: Merriam-Webster, Inc. pp. 613.

Mezrich, J.J. (1994). "When Is a Tree a Hedge?" *Financial Analysts Journal.* 50 (Nov./Dec.): 75–81.

Mieczkowski, Z. (1985). "The Tourism Climatic Index: A Method of Evaluating World Climates for Tourism." *The Canadian Geographer.* 29 (3): 220–33.

Minns, C.K., Cairns, V.W., and Randall R.G. (1994). "An Index of Biotic Integrity (IBI) for Fish Assemblages in the Littoral Zone of Great Lakes' Areas of Concern." *Canadian Journal of Fisheries and Aquatic Sciences.* 51:1804–22.

Mirloup, J. (1974). "Elements methodoliques pour une etude de l'equipment hotelier: L'exemple des departments de la Loire moyenne." *No Rois.* 83: 443–452.

Morley, C.L. (1994). "The Use of CPI for Tourism Prices in Demand Modelling." *Tourism Management.* 15(5): 342-346.

Murphy, P.E. (1992). "Data Gathering for Community-Oriented Tourism Planning: Case Study of Vancouver Island, British Columbia," *Leisure Studies.* 11(1): 65–79.

New York Times. (1994). "U.S. Index Signals Slower Growth in '95." *New York Times.* (Late New York Edition) (Dec. 30) p. D16.

O'Leary, J.T., Hsieh, S., Uysal, M., and Bailie, G. (1993). "Indexing High Propensity Travel in Canada." *Proceeding of TTRA 24th Annual Conference,* Whistler, British Columbia, Canada (June 13–16, 1993).

Oppermann, M. (1992a). "International Tourist Flows in Malaysia." *Annals of Tourism Research.* 19(3): 482–500.

Oppermann, M. (1992b). "Travel Dispersal Index." *The Journal of Tourism Studies.* 3 (1): 44–49.

Oppermann, M. (1993). "Regional Market Segmentation Analysis in Australia." *Journal of Travel & Tourism Marketing.* 2(4): 59–74.

Pearce, D.G. (1987). *Tourism Today: A Geographical Analysis.* New York: Longman.

Pearce, D.G., and Elliott, J.M.C. (1983). "The Spatial Structure of Tourist Accommodation and Hotel Demand in Spain." *Geoforum.* 16: 37–50.

Peralta, J.M., Arnold, A.M., and Currie, W.D. (1994). "Effects of Testosterone on Skeletal Growth in Lambs as Assesses by Labeling Index of Chondrocytes in the Metacarpal Bone Growth Plate." *Journal of Animal Science.* 72: 2629–34.

Philipsson, J., Banos, G., and Arnason, T. (1994). "Present and Future Uses of Selection Index Methodology in Dairy Cattle." *Journal of Dairy Science.* 77: 3252–61.

Pott, T.D. and Uysal, M. (1992). "Tourism Intensity as a Function of Accommodations," *Journal of Travel Research.* 31(2): 18–21.

Quayson, J., and Var, T. (1982). "A Tourism Demand Function for Okanagan, BC," *Tourism Management.* 3(June): 108–115.

Rafferty, M.D. (1990). "The Effects of Instruction in Geography on College Students' Perception of World Regions as Tourism Destinations," *Tourism Recreation Research.* 15(2): 30–40.

Restaurant Business, Inc. (1994). "Growing Places—The Ultimate Guide to Pitching a New Restaurant Market." *Restaurant Business.* 93/14: 34–42.

Ross, J. H. "A Measure of Site Attraction" (Ottawa, Environment Canada, Occasional Paper No. 2 (reprint), 1973).

Royer, L.E., McCool, S.F., and Hunt, J.D. (1974). "The Relative Importance of Tourism to State Economies." *Journal of Travel Research.* 14 (3): 13–16.

Sanders, T.B., Beard, S.J., Levesque, D., and Smith III, G. (1993). "A New Index for Tourism: The Case of Maine and the Canadian Provinces." *Journal of Travel Research.* 32(fall): 49–53.

SAS Institute. (1980). *SAS/ETS User's Guide.* Cary, NC: SAS Institute. pp. 6.1–6.23.

Schmidhause, H.P. (1975). "Travel Propensity and Travel Frequency." In Burkart, A.J. and Medlik, J. (eds.), *The Management of Tourism.* London: Heinemann.

Schmidhause, H.P. (1976). "The Swiss Travel Market and Its Role within the Main Tourism Generating Countries of Europe." *Tourist Review.* 31: 15–18.

Sharpe, W.F. (1966). "Mutual Fund Performance." *Journal of Business.* 39 (6): 119–138.

Shiskin, J., Young, A.H., and Musgrave, J.C. (1976). *The X-11 Variant of the Census Method II Seasonal Adjustment Program.* Washington, DC: U.S. Department of Commerce, Bureau of Economic Analysis. (Report BEA-R 76-01. Available from National Technical Information Service as PB-261 432).

Silber, J. (1989). "Factor Components, population Subgroups and the Computation of the Gini Index of Inequality." *The Review of Economics and Statistics.* 71 (Feb.): 107–15.

Sissors, J.Z. and Surmanek, J. (1982). *Advertising Media Planning* (2nd ed.). pp 131–133.

Smith, S.L.J. (1995). *Tourism Analysis: A Handbook.* New York: Longman, Harlow.

Statistics Canada. (1980). *The X-II-ARIMA Seasonal Adjustment Method.* Statistics Canada—Cat. No. 12-564E Occassional. Ottawa, Ontario: Statistics Canada.

Statistics Canada. (1985). *The Travel Price Index Reference Paper.* Travel, Tourism and Recreation Section of the, Education, Culture and Tourism Division. Ottawa, Ontario: Statistics Canada.

Statistics Canada. (1994). *International Travel: Travel between Canada and Other Countries 1993.* Statistics Canada—Cat. No. 66-201 Annual. Ottawa, Ontario: Statistics Canada.

Statistics Canada. (1996a). *National Tourism Indicators, First Quarter 1996.* Statistics Canada—Cat. No. 13-009-XPB Annual. Ottawa, Ontario: Statisitcs Canada.

Statistics Canada. (1996b). *National Tourism Indicators, Sources and Methods 1996.* Statistics Canada—Cat. No. 13-594-GPE. Ottawa, Ontario: Statistics Canada.

Stevenson, R.W. (1995). "Markets Shaken as a British Bank Takes a Big Loss." *New York Times.* (Late New York Edition) (Feb. 27) p. A1+.

Stynes, D.J. (1978). "The Peaking Problem in Outdoor Recreation: Measurement and Analysis." Unpublished paper presented at the Annual Meeting of the National Recreation and Parks Association, Miami, Florida.

Tang, J.C.S. and Rochananond, N. (1991). "Attractiveness as a Tourist Destination: A Comparative Study of Thailand and Selected Countries." *Socio-Economic Planning Science.* 242: 229–236.

Taylor, P.J. (1977). *Quantitative methods in geography.* Boston: Houghton Mifflin. pp. 58–65.

"Big MacCurrencies," (1995). *Economist.* (April 15): 74.

Thompson, P.T. (1971). "The Use of Mountain Recreational Resources: A Comparison of Recreation and Tourism in the Colorado Rockies and the Swiss Alps." Boulder: University of Colorado.

Tierney, P.T. (1990). "Development and Application of a State Tourism Tracking Index." Paper presented at NRPA Symposium on Leisure Research, October 12–15, Phoenix, Arizona.

Treynor, J.L. (1965). "How to Rate Management Investment Funds." *Harvard Business Review.* 44 (1): 63–75.

Uchitelle, L. (1995). "Labor Costs Show Small Increase." *New York Times.* (late New York Edition) (Feb. 1) p. D1+.

Underhill, L.G. (1994). "Index Numbers for Waterbird Populations. I. Review and Methodology." *The Journal of Applied Ecology.* 31(3): 463–80.

United Nations. (1976). *Statistical Yearbook 1975,* New York, pp. 67–78, pp. 544–560.

United State Department of Labor. (1966). *The Consumer Price Index: History and Techniques.* Washington, D.C.: United State Department of Labor.

United State Department of Labor. (1978). *The Consumer Price Index: Concepts and Content Over the Years.* Washington, D.C.: United State Department of Labor. (Report 517).

U.S. Travel Data Center. (1989). *The 1988–89 Economic Review of Travel in America.* Washington, D.C: U.S. Travel Data Center.

Uysal, M. and Crompton, J.L. (1984). "Determinants of Demand for International Tourist Flows to Turkey." *Tourism Management.* 288–297.

Uysal, M., and Crompton, J.L. (1985). "An Overview of Approaches Used to Forecast Tourism Demand." *Journal of Travel Research.* 25(Spring): 7–15.

Uysal, M., and Crompton, J.L. (1987). "Deriving a Relative Price Index for Inclusion in International Tourism Demand Estimation Models Revisited." *Journal of Travel Research.* 25(Spring): 40.

Uysal, M., and McDonald, C.D. (1989). "Visitor Segmentation by Trip Index." *Journal of Travel Research.* 27: 38–41.

Uysal, M., Oh, H.C. and O'Leary, J.T. (1995). "Seasonal Variation in Propensity to Travel in the U.S." *Journal of Tourism Systems and Quality Management,* 1(1):1–13.

Uysal, M., and Potts, T.D. (1990). "An Analysis of Coastal Tourism Resources with Special Reference to Accommodations: A South Carolina Study." *Proceedings of the 1990 Congress on Coastal and Marine Tourism: A Symposium and Workshop on Balancing Conservation and Economic Development,* Volume II. Honolulu, Hawaii, USA—25–31 May 1990.

Van Doren, C. (1967). *An Interaction Travel Travel Model for Projecting Attendence of Campers at Michigan State Parks.* Unpublished: Ph.D. dissertation. East Lansing: Michigan State University.

Van Doren, S.C., and Stubbles, R. (1975). "Regional Variations in the United States Summer Travel 1972," Paper presented at the 1975 American Geographers Association meeting, Wisconsin, April.

Var, T., Beck, R.A.D., and Loftus, P. (1977). "Determination of Touristic Attractiveness of the Touristic Areas in British Columbia." *Journal of Travel Research.* 15: 23–29.

Vina, L.Y., Hollas, D., Merrifield, J., and Ford, J. (1994). "A Principal Components-Based Tourism Activity Index." *Journal of Travel Research.* (Spring): 37–40.

"Morgan Initiates Index to Track Performance of South Africa Bonds." (1995). *Wall Street Journal.* (Eastern Edition) (Feb. 9) p. C6.

Wassenaar, D.J., (1989). "The Escondido Visitor Industry, 1980–1989." A Report for the Escondido Convention & Visitors Bureau, Escondido, California, April 8.

Wassenaar D.J., and Stafford E.R. (1991). "The Lodging Index: An Economic Indicator for the Hotel/Motel Industry." *Journal of Travel Research.* Summer: 18–21.

Wei, J.Z. (1995). "Empirical Tests of the Pricing of Nikkei Put Warrants." *Finance Review.* 30 (May): 211–241.

Weissmark, M.S., and Giacomo, D.A. (1994). "A Therapeutic Index: Measuring Therapeutic Actions in Psychotherapy." *Journal of Consulting and Clinical Psychology.* 62: 315–23.

Williams, A.V., and Zelinsky, W. (1970). "On Some Patterns of International Tourist Flows." *Economic Geography.* 46: 549–567.

Witt, S.F., and Martin, C.A. (1987). "Deriving a Relative Price Index for Inclusion in International Tourism Demand Estimation Models." *Journal of Travel Research.* 25: 38–40.

Wolfe, R.I. (1966). *Parameters of Recreational Travel in Ontario.* DHO Report. R B111. Downsview, Ontario: Ontario Department of Highways.

Index